W9-BGL-686

SAUDI ARABIAN
DEVELOPMENT
STRATEGY

SAUDI ARABIAN DEVELOPMENT STRATEGY

Donald A. Wells

American Enterprise Institute for Public Policy Research
Washington, D.C.

Donald A. Wells is professor of economics in the college of business and public administration at the University of Arizona.

ISBN 0-8447-3219-2

National Energy Study 12, September 1976

Library of Congress Catalog Card No. 76-27127

Printed in the United States of America

THE AEI
NATIONAL ENERGY PROJECT

The American Enterprise Institute's
National Energy Project was established in early 1974
to examine the broad array of issues
affecting U.S. energy demands and supplies.
The project commissions research into all important
ramifications of the energy problem—economic
and political, domestic and international, private
and public—and presents the results
in studies such as this one.
In addition it sponsors symposia, debates, conferences,
and workshops, some of which are televised.

The project is chaired by Melvin R. Laird,
former congressman, secretary of defense,
and domestic counsellor to the President,
and now senior counsellor of *Reader's Digest*.
The advisory council represents a wide range of
energy-related viewpoints.
Professor Edward J. Mitchell of the
University of Michigan is the project director.

Views expressed are those of the authors
and do not necessarily reflect the views of
either the advisory council and others associated with
the project or of the advisory panels,
staff, officers, and trustees of AEI.

Cover and book design: Pat Taylor

CONTENTS

1
THE FRAMEWORK
FOR ANALYSIS

The increase in the export earnings of the Organization of Petroleum Exporting Countries (OPEC) from about $30 billion in 1973 to approximately $105 billion in 1974 is one of those rare historical events that fundamentally alter economic and political relationships among nations and groups of nations. It is inevitable and desirable that these events be followed by evaluations of their political and economic consequences. It is inevitable but less desirable that the initial evaluations are often unsubstantiated by careful analysis. One reason is the difficulty of evaluating the results of change when relationships have been altered radically. Extrapolation from past data is inappropriate when the magnitude of change is great. When there is little information available and when little research has been completed on the political and economic policies and the institutions of the countries involved, the chance increases that initial responses will be based on less than adequate information. So it was for such countries as the Persian Gulf sheikhdoms, Saudi Arabia, Kuwait, and many of the other members of OPEC. Since data for most of these countries are scarce and unreliable, research has heretofore been limited.

One example of the problems posed by inadequate information is the wide range of estimates of the wealth to be accumulated within a few years by the members of OPEC as a result of the fourfold increase in the price of oil exported by these countries. The World Bank's estimate of $600 billion by 1980 was widely quoted and received early and general acceptance. The alarm was considerable,

I would like to thank Dr. Edward J. Mitchell and the American Enterprise Institute for their support of this study. Dr. Morris Adelman and Dr. Emile Nakhleh made valuable suggestions, but of course I remain responsible for the content.

1

because the implications of such holdings of international assets were substantial. "One respectable body, assuming that the accumulation would go on into the 1980's, foresaw it eventually mounting up to as much as £ 1,250 billion. Even by 1980, it was darkly calculated, OPEC would have laid its hands on a sum equal to about three-quarters of the 1974 value of all the shares traded on the world's main stock exchanges."[1] Especially during 1974 concern was expressed for the stability of the international monetary system, the ability of major oil-importing countries to pay for oil imports, and the ownership of wealth in the major industrialized countries, particularly the United States. The projected new patterns of income and wealth appeared to threaten existing international financial institutions.

The early estimates of the wealth being accumulated by the members of OPEC were rooted in a belief that the oil producers did not "need" the income and/or did not have the capacity to spend it. With time for a more careful study of the issues, analysts have revised these estimates downward, although the range in the estimates remains wide. The Morgan Guaranty Trust Company of New York estimated that OPEC holdings of external financial assets might peak by 1978 at $248 billion and decline thereafter to about $180 billion by 1980.[2] More recently, Morgan Guaranty Trust estimated that the peak holdings in 1978 or 1979 may be less than $200 billion.[3] Testifying before the Senate Foreign Relations subcommittee, Assistant Secretary of the Treasury Gerald Parsky predicted that new accumulations of oil revenue surpluses by the members of OPEC "will effectively disappear before the end of the decade, and that new investment will begin to decline before they reach a cumulative total of $200 billion to $250 billion."[4] Using what it considers to be the most plausible of its four projections, the First National City Bank of New York estimated that OPEC net assets abroad will have reached $188 billion in 1980.[5] Walter J. Levy maintained that current-account surpluses by members of OPEC will still be high in 1980 and that the OPEC cumulative surplus will total $449 billion by 1980.[6]

---

[1] "Survey," *The Economist*, May 19, 1975, p. 27.

[2] *World Financial Markets*, Morgan Guaranty Trust Company of New York, January 21, 1975, p. 8.

[3] *World Financial Markets*, October 20, 1975, p. 11.

[4] *Wall Street Journal*, March 19, 1975, p. 7.

[5] *Monthly Economic Letter*, First National City Bank of New York, June 1975.

[6] "Future OPEC Accumulation of Oil Money: A New Look at a Critical Problem," W. J. Levy Consultants Corp., New York, August 1975.

One danger is, of course, that policy makers may continue to react primarily on the basis of the more alarming statistics. These tend to make the biggest headlines and may have a lasting effect. The introduction of numerous bills in Congress to restrict foreign investment in the United States and the congressional hearings on this subject were triggered by a concern over massive investments by oil-producing countries. Thus, while the actual situation is sufficiently serious to warrant an examination of U.S. policies toward foreign investment, our responses to the situation are likely to vary considerably according to our estimates of the magnitudes involved.

Another lesson of the past year is an obvious one, but one that was not fully appreciated in the early reactions to the increased price of oil. The members of OPEC are a diverse lot, with differing political philosophies, cultural backgrounds, and economic capabilities. Generalizations about the likely behavior of these countries with respect to their potential revenues, utilization of funds, and accumulation of external financial assets hide a diversity of interests, capabilities, and potential experiences. More careful country-by-country studies will provide a firmer foundation for policy analysis than generalizations about OPEC as a group.

In addition to these reasons for studying each country individually, there are special reasons for focusing on Saudi Arabia. Its petroleum reserves are estimated to be about 170 billion barrels. As the world's third largest producer of crude oil, following the Soviet Union and the United States, its petroleum earnings are the largest in the OPEC group. Given its stage of development and its relatively small population, it has shown considerable discretion in its attitudes toward maximizing and utilizing its present revenues.

An analysis of Saudi Arabia's development plans is a major key to an assessment of the effect of its revenues on the rest of the world. The pace and direction of Saudi development will be influential in determining the price and availability of oil, in shaping political developments in the Middle East and elsewhere, and in modifying the structures of major industries and international financial markets. While the principal effects of development strategy will be experienced directly by the Saudis, the emergence of Saudi Arabia as a relatively wealthy nation capable of exerting appreciable international economic influence makes its plans and expectations of interest to us all. For example, if modest investment programs were part of their current investment program, the Saudis might regard their country's current petroleum revenues as excessive, and there might be less incentive to increase or even maintain current levels of petroleum

3

production. Similarly, if the Saudis were to anticipate a continuing and total reliance upon oil exports for their economic well-being, current pricing and production decisions concerning oil would be shaped by this anticipation. On the other hand, if major industrial development were to be pushed, Saudi requirements for current revenues would increase and the rate of exploitation of Saudi petroleum resources would be accelerated. A study of Saudi Arabian development strategy will illuminate these and other points.

Potential Revenues

The development plans of Saudi Arabia cannot reasonably be assessed unless there is general agreement on the likely level of Saudi government revenues over the next decade. While any estimates of revenues over this period are speculative—and while it is not useful to attempt to be precise in these estimates because too many factors can intervene in the calculations—the fact that the estimation of revenues may be somewhat arbitrary will not appreciably affect the results of our analysis. First, Saudi Arabia has a greater opportunity to stabilize its revenues than do most oil exporters. Second, the development plans of Saudi Arabia will depend as much on the level of revenues that Saudi officials anticipate as on the level of revenues realized, unless the realized revenues diverge considerably from those anticipated.

There is a strong possibility that revenues will be stabilized because of the existing flexibility in setting petroleum production levels in Saudi Arabia and because of the predominant role of Saudi Arabia in determining the world price of petroleum, particularly during the next five years. In the production of petroleum, there seems to be no technical restraint that would prevent the Saudis from increasing capacity to 18–20 million barrels a day by 1980. By August 1973, just before the embargo, Saudi Arabia's output averaged 8.5 million barrels a day. At that time, Aramco had plans to expand its capacity to about 11.5 million barrels a day. Some were estimating at that time a capacity of as much as 20 million barrels a day by 1980.[7] Minister of Petroleum Sheikh Ahmed Zaki Yamani had made statements before the embargo that 20 million barrels a day was a realistic goal. Aramco had planned capacity increases of approximately 80 percent in the 1973–75 period, and it did not seem unreasonable for Yamani to project an additional 80–100 percent increase over the

---

[7] *Oil and Gas Journal*, December 25, 1972, pp. 82-83.

subsequent five-year period. By mid-1976, capacity was approximately 12 million barrels a day, and the Saudis were reported to be "encouraging their friends, the oil companies, working as their contractors to increase capacity in Saudi Arabia by another 25 percent to nearly 16 million barrels a day."[8]

Technologically, then, more than doubling the production of petroleum would be feasible. However, the maintenance of the higher international price of crude oil has been rooted in the willingness of the major producers to restrict production. Because of its size, Saudi Arabia has played a key part in the determination of OPEC strategy: in 1975 Saudi production averaged only 6.8 million barrels a day, a decline of nearly 17 percent from 1974.[9] With the artificial restriction of output probably a permanent feature of pricing policies, it is not likely in the near future that Saudi Arabia will utilize its full capacity. Production will be geared to the overall pricing and marketing strategy of OPEC. The existence of installed capacity of more than 15 million barrels a day, however, will give Saudi Arabia broad options in its production and pricing policies.

Like production estimates, forecasts of the price of Saudi crude oil during the next five to ten years are speculative. The energy policies of individual countries and international political relationships have to be specified to arrive at an accurate forecast. If we remember these problems, it is not unreasonable to assume that in constant dollars the price of crude oil will be maintained throughout the 1975–80 period. The increase of 10 percent in petroleum prices announced by OPEC in September 1975 was justified by the oil producers as an attempt to maintain the real price of oil. The political pressures on Saudi Arabia to maintain this established policy are considerable, and there is no indication that the Saudi leadership is willing to break with the policy. Politically, the other oil producers and non-oil-exporting Arab countries have more instruments of pressure to apply to Saudi Arabia than do the major consuming countries. Geographical proximity, religious and cultural ties, and the potential for subversion give rise to greater political leverage than the blandishments of the West.

It appears that, regardless of the prices at which crude oil is sold, Saudi Arabia is more likely to stabilize its revenues at current levels than are the other oil producers. (Saudi Arabia has, for example, allowed Iraq to increase output.) Because of its strong production position, Saudi Arabia not only can have the deciding voice in deter-

---

[8] *The Economist*, August 30, 1975, p. 63.
[9] *Petroleum Economist*, February 1976, p. 73.

mining the price of petroleum, but also, in the event that the price does begin to fall, is in the best position of any member of OPEC to increase its output and sales. Of course, Saudi Arabia's dominant production position within OPEC means that it must take into account the price effect of its production policy more than any other member of OPEC. Given this dominant position, its policies to maximize and/or to stabilize its revenues can come very close to being the policy of OPEC itself. Of all the countries in OPEC, Saudi Arabia seems to be in the best position to maintain its revenues over a wide range of future prices for petroleum. Other members of OPEC do not have the oil reserves or the technical capacity to increase production that Saudi Arabia does. Some, like Kuwait, have already restricted production to conserve their scarce reserves.

It seems reasonable to estimate that between 1975 and 1980, Saudi government revenues from the production and sale of crude oil will average between $20 and $30 billion in 1974 dollars. Because Saudi Arabia is producing well below its capacity, because there is no indication that the price will come down appreciably during the near term, and because the economic recovery in the industrial West and Japan has increased the demand for petroleum, Saudi revenues are more likely to go higher rather than lower.

Twenty to thirty billion dollars is a wide range for an estimate of future revenues. For the purpose of this analysis, however, such a range does not present major difficulties. Whatever strategy for development is adopted is likely to be consistent with either the higher or lower figure. One reason is that revenues of $20 billion are more than adequate to allow Saudi Arabia to undertake a massive program of development that requires expenditures greater than those that could actually be implemented. Since Saudi petroleum revenues were only $1.4 billion in 1970 and about $5 billion in 1973, $20 billion a year appear to be more than sufficient for any likely development plans. Second, the increase in revenues from $5 billion to $20 billion should result in a high level of saving by the government. If revenues fluctuate in the $20 billion to $30 billion range, undoubtedly it will be the level of saving that will change, not the likely level of spending. Thus, while the rate of economic growth may change according to the exact level of petroleum revenues, development plans should be consistent with any level of revenues within the estimated range. The cumulative revenues for Saudi Arabia will approach $120 billion to $180 billion during the 1975–80 period, and the Saudi planners are unlikely to alter basic strategy merely because revenues fall toward the lower rather than the upper limit of this range.

The Continuity of Development Policy

In May 1975 Saudi Arabia's Council of Ministers approved a five-year economic plan calling for the expenditure of $143 billion. The plan is ambitious; it anticipates a growth rate of over 13 percent a year for the output of goods and services (excluding the petroleum sector). Investment is to be directed into all sectors of the economy—agriculture, industry, mining, and development of water resources—and expenditures for transportation, communication, and electricity will be large. Social welfare programs, such as those aimed at the improvement of health and education, will be expanded considerably. This new five-year plan provides a glimpse of the pattern of development that is likely to emerge in Saudi Arabia during the next few decades. Nevertheless while the plan is revealing, it is hazardous to reach judgments concerning development strategy on the basis of this plan alone.

Right now, the plan should be viewed primarily as a summary of the claims on the new national wealth advanced by the various ministries. During the implementation of the plan, some claims will very likely be denied and others expanded considerably. For those who associate five-year plans with the development process in the Soviet Union, the document prepared by the Saudi Ministry of Planning might better be called a shopping list.

Because the new development plan does not clearly establish priorities, one way of gaining insight into Saudi development strategy is first to study the past decade of development. During this decade, when Saudi financial resources were much smaller, major policy choices had to be made and priorities established.

Some might argue that the record of Saudi Arabian policy in the past would offer little insight into future Saudi policy because of the increased opportunities afforded by the lack of any short-run financial or foreign-exchange constraints on projects and programs. In this respect, it is quite reasonable to expect to find priority being given to new projects that were not feasible earlier because of a lack of financial resources. But it is useful to differentiate between the expansion of existing programs and fundamentally new strategies for economic development. In this study it is judged likely that the major outlines of Saudi development policy of the past decade will persist into the next. The new wealth of the Saudis is not likely to result in a marked departure from earlier policies. The reasons are:

- The continuity of policies associated with the dominance of the royal family and the political stability that it brings.

7

- The limits to the direction of future development imposed by the geography and the natural resources of Saudi Arabia.
- The relatively small population and the scarcity of skills in the indigenous population, which limit options.
- The pervasive continuing influence of Islam and Saudi culture in shaping development strategy.
- The predominant role of the government in the national economy.

Political Stability. For almost fifty years the Saud family has maintained its control over the kingdom that bears its name. Before the establishment of the Saud hegemony, various tribes had ruled for different periods, but each had been deposed in turn in the tribal warfare that had historically characterized the Arabian Peninsula. It is no coincidence that the period of dominance by the Saud family has coincided with the development of petroleum resources. The leverage afforded by oil income had a profound effect on the relationships between the many tribal families and was a strong element in cementing the kingdom. The loyalty of both friends and former enemies has long been cultivated by cash payments made possible by the petroleum royalties and income taxes paid to the king.

Today, the royal family is a diverse group, of which perhaps 200 or 300 out of a total of more than 3,000 princes constitute a form of political party and exercise administrative control over the affairs of the kingdom. Following the assassination of King Faisal, the smooth succession of King Khalid and Crown Prince Fahd demonstrated the supremacy of the royal family. The existence of the formal absolute monarchy should not obscure the political process that produces a consensus among the members of the royal family, the leaders of other tribes, and the few persons not belonging to the family (such as Sheikh Yamani) who participate in policy decisions. While one should not rule out the possibility that a radical regime could seize power, there is little evidence of active political opposition to the dominance of the royal family. There was a greater threat of radical seizure of power during the 1950s and 1960s, when President Nasser of Egypt looked covetously at the oil riches of the peninsula. Today, with the kingdom's vast oil wealth at their disposal, the political leaders of Saudi Arabia are better able to mute any opposition, internal or external, with their largesse.

Far-reaching as the individual power and influence of King Faisal were, it is important to understand that his authority seemed to rest partly on his willingness to share decision-making processes. While Saudi Arabia has few of the political institutions of Western democracy, political authority in Saudi Arabia does depend upon the ruler's ability to respond to the mixture of interests of such groups as the extended royal family, the Bedouins, the various religious groups, and the educated civil servants. Government policies in Saudi Arabia emerge from a mixture of diverse interests similar to those in the societies that call themselves democratic. These processes survive the person who is king at any given moment, and they give a higher degree of stability to policy goals than many outsiders might expect to find. The dominance of the Saud family imparts political stability, which is accompanied by a high degree of stability in economic policy.

Geography. The geography and climate of Saudi Arabia impose stringent limitations on the range of feasible alternatives of the Saudi planners. The area of Saudi Arabia is over one million square miles, about one-third the size of the continental United States. The kingdom constitutes almost four-fifths of the Arabian Peninsula. The hot dry climate produces temperatures above 120 degrees in the summer and in much of the kingdom annual precipitation averaging about three inches. The principal exception to the dry climate is the mountainous Asir region of the southwest corner of Saudi Arabia, where annual rainfall approaches twenty inches. The central plateau, the Najd, is arid, except for the area around the capital city, Riyadh, which has springs and an abundance of well water, and scattered oases such as Buraydah and Hayil. The Rub al-Khali, the Empty Quarter, is just that—the empty quarter. Comprising the central southern quarter of the kingdom and the largest desert in the world, it has no permanent residents.

One major consequence of Saudi geography is that there are only three population centers in the kingdom. In the western region are the commercial city of Jeddah and the religious cities of Mecca and Medina. In the Najd is the capital city of Riyadh, with perhaps 500,000 residents. On the east coast are the cities of Al-Khobar and Dammam, as well as Dhahran, the city constructed to house the American employees of Aramco. Just west of the cities on the east coast are the two oasis settlements of Hofuf and Haradh. Whatever industrial development takes place will tend to be concentrated in the Jeddah region on the west coast and in the Dammam and Al-Khobar area on the east coast.

A second major consequence of Saudi geography and climate is that the opportunities for agricultural development are limited. Saudi Arabia is a net importer of food, and when rising incomes result in more diversified tastes, increasing quantities of food will be imported, particularly to the urbanized areas. Less than 0.2 percent of the total land area is cropped, and efforts to expand this area appreciably would be very costly.

Since agriculture and animal husbandry support more than half the population at not much more than subsistence level, any effort to improve employment opportunities for this portion of the population would require the transfer of a substantial proportion of the labor force from agriculture to other sectors of the economy. Development policy cannot rely upon agriculture to provide much opportunity for employment or for rising incomes of the type implied by a rate of economic growth of over 10 percent a year.

Population. The few population centers in the kingdom are partially a result of geography, but they are also a reflection of the relatively small size of the population. Out of a total population of approximately 5 million persons, the labor force numbers about 1.5 million. Of the total labor force perhaps as many as 600,000 are foreign, most of them unskilled workers from the Yemen. Agriculture's share of the labor force is close to half, and perhaps as much as 20 percent of the labor force is employed in the public sector. Thus a small proportion of the total labor force is employed in the industrial, commercial, construction, and service sectors. This relatively small labor force limits the alternatives for economic development.

Options are also limited by the fact that there are relatively few skilled workers among the labor force. The systematic training of Saudis as a part of government policy began only a decade ago. Initial efforts concentrated on the education of government employees, primarily through scholarships to enable them to attend foreign universities, and the establishment of the Institute of Public Administration in Riyadh, which has provided training in English and in various job skills for more than 10,000 government employees. While some vocational training has been provided through six training centers, fewer than 4,000 persons have been graduated from these centers, so the effect thus far on the skills available in the labor force has been minimal. The structure and pace of Saudi economic development is conditioned by the lack of skills in the labor force more than by any other factor. A key issue is the extent to which the Saudi government is willing to utilize and to absorb foreign skilled workers. The pace of any effort at industrialization will be retarded if there is too great a dependence upon the domestic labor force.

Culture. The efforts of the Saudi leaders to integrate development plans with Saudi tradition and Islam complicate development plans. Political leaders in Saudi Arabia have always attempted to limit the influence of the intrusion represented by the American oil community brought in by Aramco. The founder of the country, King Abdul-Aziz ibn Saud, tried to restrict the cultural influence of the American oil personnel to the eastern province. The political life and the religious life of the kingdom he founded were fundamentally intertwined, and he feared the potential political consequences of changing traditional beliefs and customs. His strong commitment to Islam was also an important element of his attitude toward modernization.

King Faisal shared many of these attitudes, and while he played a vital role in initiating institutional changes, he, too, attempted to accommodate the process of political and economic development to the desire to retain essential elements of Saudi culture and religion.[10] These concerns still predominate, but there are two reasons for believing that they may receive less attention in the future than they have in the past. One is that, in spite of the caution exercised in the past, exposure to Western attitudes and technology has already altered many of the attitudes and customs upon which Saudi life has been based. Now these influences will be heightened by the increased magnitude of revenues and expenditures, and it is doubtful that changes in culture can be avoided to any appreciable extent. The other reason is that while it is too early to make a judgment, there are indications that King Khalid and Crown Prince Fahd are amenable to acceptance of the cultural consequences of a rapid development effort.

Government. Saudi government expenditures and revenues have averaged 60 percent of gross domestic product (GDP) in recent years, and the stimulus and initiative for most other forms of economic activity rest with the government. Either through taxation of foreign companies or through its ownership of oil-production facilities, the Saudi government's role in the petroleum sector guarantees its continued dominance of all economic activity.

Regardless of the forms of property ownership in the various sectors of the economy, the government will dominate economic activity by establishing the levels and composition of investment and

---

10 One of the overt signs of the type of accommodation that occurs is the construction of a mosque next to a highly automated cement factory that was put up in an isolated area. In this way the Saudis' practice of prayer five times a day can be reconciled with the utilization of labor in a highly automated factory.

11

consumption. The Saudi authorities regard petroleum and the ancillary activities of producers of petroleum as national resources to be exploited for national development and for improving the economic well-being of the citizens. The commitment of the Saudi authorities to private ownership of property in other sectors of the economy should not obscure the domination of the economy by the government. Most major industries have been established with Saudi government equity participation. Petromin, the state enterprise, dominates all industrial activities in the downstream operations of the petroleum industry, including those, such as the chemical and fertilizer industries, that utilize petroleum and natural gas as sources of energy and raw material. Even where there is complete private ownership of business, government subsidies, requirements for import licenses, and other governmental regulatory powers will exercise decisive influence. It is doubtful that any major private business activity could be initiated or could survive without explicit or implicit government approval.

These characteristics provide a strong basis for continuity in Saudi development policy. By examining programs and economic development of the past decade, it is possible to identify the major elements of Saudi development plans during this period. Then Saudi policies since the end of 1973 can be compared with those of the earlier period to assess the effect of the increase in oil revenues on development. Finally, an assessment can be made of the international implications of these policies.

2
THE PREVIOUS EXPERIENCE

It is widely accepted that Saudi Arabia is unprepared for the efficient use of all its new wealth. In addition, some might judge that Saudi Arabia does not "need" its large income. Both views imply that Saudi Arabia will save a major portion of its income, and the estimates of large foreign-exchange holdings and foreign investments by Saudi Arabia are at least partially predicated upon this implication. Similarly, these views suggest that Saudi Arabia can afford to be capricious and cavalier in its policies toward the production and sale of petroleum and in its actions in foreign-exchange markets. These views will also have important effects on the pattern and pace of development. As a part of the investigation of Saudi development strategy, it is important to determine the extent to which "need" and the ability to utilize the higher revenues efficiently affect Saudi policies.

Need

The question whether Saudi Arabia "needs" its new level of income and wealth is not of much economic significance. If "need" is defined as a level of living providing for minimal or moderate standards of food, clothing, and shelter, then it is true that Saudi Arabia does not need all its new wealth. Even here there might be difficulties in arriving at a consensus as to what constitutes minimal or moderate standards. This problem aside, it is doubtful whether individuals or societies in the industrialized West would accept an assertion that they do not require the levels of income that afford them a standard of living greater than what is commonly accepted as minimal or adequate. For most individuals, attempts to improve material well-being and to obtain cultural amenities require noticeably higher levels of income than those associated with need. It is condescending of westerners to reach a judgment that the people of the oil-exporting countries should aspire to less than they and others in their own societies do. At present, a major share of the population of Saudi Arabia lives at or near subsistence levels. It will take a considerable effort to mobilize Saudi Arabian resources, financial and otherwise, to provide for a sustained and substantial increase in Saudi living standards. The present high levels of revenues and the potential growth in domestic product and incomes should not cause us to overlook the fact that there are large numbers of poor persons and families in Saudi Arabia. Moreover, in whatever manner and direction their desires are determined and expressed, it is the Saudis alone who should judge the adequacy of revenues, output, and income.

In interpreting the attitudes of Saudi policy makers, it is advisable to place more emphasis on their actions than on their public statements. In the confrontation between petroleum importers and exporters, the exporters find it to their advantage to stress the point that the importers have more to lose by disruptions of supply than do the producers. Also, to improve their bargaining position, exporters such as Saudi Arabia find it advantageous to express their willingness to accept reduced revenues from lower output and sales. For these reasons, it is appropriate to discount the public statements of such officials as Sheikh Ahmed Zaki Yamani (the minister of petroleum), which suggest that Saudi Arabia would be content with much lower revenues and is sacrificing by providing for the petroleum requirements of the industrialized countries. Undoubtedly Saudi Arabia could adjust to revenues lower than the forecast range of $20 billion to $30 billion. This is quite different from saying that they do not need the income and would be better off with lower revenues.

Absorption Capacity

The capital-absorptive capacity of a less developed country—that is, its ability to utilize investment capital efficiently—is likely to be limited, largely because of the lack of complementary factors of production. Transportation and communication facilities may not be adequately developed—that is, after all, what "less developed" means. Very often the establishment of a new enterprise requires certain raw materials that may not be available in sufficient quantities. Similarly, other semifinished products may be necessary inputs to the new production process. But most important, a new facility requires managerial talents and technical skills. The lack of sufficient complementary labor inputs can often make it impossible to use new plant and equipment effectively. Thus,

> Every economist would agree that in any country there is some limit to the rate of capital formation that can be carried out at any given time with a resulting increase in productivity. There are technical and other limitations. Among the technical ones are the size of the construction industry, the availability of materials for capital construction and of workers for construction and subsequent operation, the capacity of the ports and transportation system to carry capital goods, of the communication system to carry messages, of the country's housing to house expatriate or migrant builders and workers, and of the existing productive complex into which or onto which the new enterprises must be fitted and on which they must depend in part for their productivity. Other limitations would include the number of individuals in the society with adequate managerial and technical capabilities, including in the extreme case the capability of making contracts with foreigners to do the capital formation, and the values and motivations of many groups in the society: of workers, which affect their availability for new enterprises; of government officials, which will determine the degree of waste, corruption, and misdirection of investment. . . .[1]

Saudi Arabia faces all these problems, but whether they will limit development expenditures to a level far below that intended by Saudi planners is not certain. One reason for uncertainty is that the idea of absorption capacity has only limited relevance to the situation in which Saudi Arabia finds itself. The government of Saudi Arabia earns a high proportion of the total national income, and it is not immediately necessary for the government to direct its revenues primarily into productive investment. If approximately half the Saudi national income is earned by the government, investment as a percentage of total output and income can reach a respectable 20 to 25 percent and still allow for half the total revenue to be spent in ways other than productive investment. It is a mistake to associate capital-absorptive capacity with limits to the ability of the government to increase its spending rapidly. In other words, it is not unreasonable to expect that at least half of Saudi government expenditures may be for consumption rather than for investment. With no foreign-

---

[1] Everett E. Hagan, *The Economics of Development* (Homewood, Ill.: Richard D. Irwin, Inc., 1975), pp. 430-431.

exchange constraint on the potential level of imports at present, and with eager sellers of goods pressing their wares, government spending can increase very rapidly, unless the government attempts to limit the rise in standards of consumption.

In this respect, it is helpful to differentiate between capital-absorptive capacity and what might be labeled expenditures-absorptive capacity. It is too narrow a view of the development process to limit consideration to investment expenditures only. Saudi development plans must ultimately be related to the material well-being of the Saudis. In the particular circumstances of Saudi Arabia, where high rates of investment can be maintained at the same time that standards of consumption are rising rapidly, expenditures to increase present consumption are an inherent part of development strategy, just as are expenditures made for the purpose of increasing future consumption. In an important sense, rising standards of consumption now are the dividends on the policies of the previous thirty years, which encouraged the exploitation and development of the petroleum sector. That this investment was undertaken in the private sector and was done by foreign companies makes it no less a part of development strategy than investments made by the government itself. Development strategy is not a post-1973 phenomenon. Again, additional insight into the future Saudi experience is likely to be achieved if we put today's policies into the context of past experience and policies. We may ask where Saudi Arabia would be today if it had excluded foreign investors throughout the past thirty years. Regardless of the circumstances which brought about increases in the price of oil and the subsequent increase in the government's revenues from petroleum, Saudi Arabia would not now be initiating a huge increase both in investment and in consumption expenditures if the capacity to produce crude oil had not already been installed.

A discussion of Saudi Arabian development plans should include all categories of spending. By virtue of its claim to the income generated by the petroleum sector the government plays the major role in determining the economic well-being of the people. The level and composition of spending for consumption in Saudi Arabia are largely determined by government policies and government expenditures. If a discussion of Saudi Arabian development strategy focused only on investment expenditures, it would neglect one of the principal policy decisions facing Saudi authorities: the choice of the relative amounts of present or future consumption. The revenues earned by the Saudi government can be committed to expenditures for consumption, to investment, and to savings (in the form of the accumulation of both short-term and long-term foreign assets). It is the unique experience of the Saudi Arabian government to have unparalleled discretionary income. During the past five to eight years Kuwait has had an opportunity similar to that of Saudi Arabia, but Kuwait's income has not been of the magnitude of Saudi Arabia's. The same can be said of some of the Persian Gulf sheikhdoms. Countries such as Iran and Venezuela, with high levels of petroleum revenues, have much larger populations and already have had to curtail some planned expenditures because expenditures have outpaced revenues. Thus, a treatment of Saudi Arabian development plans should include all types of expenditures, rather than concentrating on investment expenditure alone.

1960–1971

In 1970 a five-year plan for development was approved by the Council of Ministers and the king. Its general objectives were to maintain Saudi "religious and moral values, and to raise the living standards and welfare of its people, while providing for national security and maintaining economic and social stability." [2] The adoption of the plan essentially represented a formalization of economic policy that had existed since the mid 1960s. In preparing the plan, the various ministries were asked to review their programs and policies, and the planning process offered the several ministries an opportunity to coordinate their activities when it was appropriate for them to do so. As stated by the Central Planning Organization,

> The purpose of the Plan is to provide a rational and orderly approach to achieving the nation's development objectives. The Plan was not intended to be a rigid, restrictive set of rules and regulations but a means of bringing increased rationality into public sector programs by establishing priorities and integrating activities to avoid bottlenecks and ensure coordination. [3]

By studying the basic elements of the plan and the developments in the Saudi economy in recent years, we can determine and assess basic economic development plans. The emphasis in this analysis is on what has happened rather than on statements of intentions. Two periods will be studied: first the decade of the 1960s and then the period from 1971 to 1975, during which revenues increased more rapidly on a sustained basis.

[2] *Report of the Central Planning Organization*, 1974, p. 17.
[3] Ibid., p. 17.

In any description of the Saudi economy, it should be emphasized that there are no consistent time-series data for the period from 1960 to the present. Governmental and nongovernmental sources give conflicting data without explanation. The recent data are more reliable than the data for the 1960s. Statistics on the petroleum sector and the foreign sector are the most reliable. For data on government expenditures, appropriations are more reliable than actual expenditures. Budget statistics for the early 1960s are not complete and were often changed without explanation. During the fiscal years for which budgets were prepared, expenditures and appropriations were at times changed by royal decree, and these changes often did not appear in published data.

All data are presented by calendar year. Many of the Saudi government data used in this study are presented according to the Islamic calendar, which is based on the lunar year (354 days with eleven leap years of 355 days each cycle of thirty years): The first year of this calendar is the year that the Prophet Muhammad emigrated from Mecca to Medina (A.D. 622); the Saudi fiscal year of 1389/90, for example, corresponds to Gregorian calendar dates September 13, 1969, to August 31, 1970. Statistics presented for the Gregorian calendar year are those for the approximately corresponding Islamic year; as an example, data for 1389/90 are presented as 1970.

Official exchange rates, given below for selected years, are used to convert riyals to U.S. dollars: [4]

1959	$1 = 3.750 riyals
1960–71	1 = 4.500
1972	1 = 4.145
1973	1 = 3.730
1974	1 = 3.550
1975	1 = 3.470

These correspond to the market rate for each period. The rate given for 1975 is the rate for summer 1975.

Economic Growth. During the 1960s, real gross domestic product for Saudi Arabia averaged an annual increase of approximately 10 percent. In 1971 the rate of growth was 13 percent.

The rate of growth is explained almost entirely by the performance of the petroleum sector. Following the Arab-Israeli war of 1967, the petroleum output of Saudi Arabia dropped, with subsequent

[4] International Monetary Fund, *International Financial Statistics*, 1960-1975.

declines in the rate of increase of oil revenues. As a result, real gross domestic product increased by only 8.1 percent in 1968 and 6.8 percent in 1969. When petroleum output increased by 15 percent in 1970 and 20 percent in 1971, real gross domestic product increased by 9.5 percent and then by an extraordinary 13.4 percent, respectively. By 1971, oil accounted for 56 percent of gross domestic product.

No other sector of the economy contributes more than a small proportion of national output. As examples, by 1971 petroleum refining accounted for almost 7 percent, transportation and communications almost 7 percent, public administration and defense 6 percent, wholesale and retail trade 6 percent, agriculture 5 percent, and construction 4 percent.[5]

Capital Formation. In the five-year period from 1966 to 1971, capital formation averaged 20 percent of gross domestic product. In light of the rapid expansion of gross domestic product during this period, it is evident that investment increased substantially, inasmuch as capital formation was more than a third higher in 1971 than it was in 1966.

If government enterprises are included in the private sector (as they are in Saudi government statistics), by 1971 the private sector accounted for almost 60 percent of total investment, and the public sector accounted for the other 40 percent. Construction accounted for almost three-fourths of total capital formation; almost 30 percent of total construction was for residences.

Manufacturing. The manufacturing sector, like all others, is dominated by the petroleum sector. Nonoil manufacturing accounted for less than 7 percent of private nonoil gross domestic product in 1971. If petroleum refining were to be excluded, manufacturing accounted for less than 2 percent of gross domestic product. In this sector, cement accounts for approximately half of paid-up capital. The output of carbonated beverages is the next largest component of manufacturing.

Overall, there were 294 manufacturing establishments in the kingdom in 1971.[6] Twenty-two firms accounted for over 90 percent of capital investment. Oil refining is the largest subsector within manufacturing. Between 1966 and 1971, the value of the output of refined petroleum increased by 64 percent. By the end of 1971, Saudi

[5] Saudi Arabian Monetary Agency [SAMA], *Annual Report 1975* (Riyadh), pp. 130-131.
[6] *Report of the Central Planning Organization*, 1974, p. 98.

Arabia had sufficient refining capacity to meet the requirements of the domestic market.

The foreign contribution to capital investment in the manufacturing sector is significant. By the beginning of 1971, seventy-five firms had been granted licenses by the Ministry of Commerce and Industry. For the most part, foreign investors maintained majority interest in their firms.

In 1971 fewer than 13,000 persons were employed in manufacturing. The largest enterprises, concentrated in the petroleum and chemicals sector, are capital-intensive operations and offered only limited employment opportunities. The 40 to 50 percent of the manufacturing labor force that is unskilled is employed primarily in the food-and-beverage industry. Skilled workers are concentrated primarily in chemicals and petroleum.

Agriculture. Growth in real output has been slowest in the agricultural sector. Throughout the 1960s, agricultural output grew at an annual rate of about 2 percent. By 1971, agriculture's share of gross domestic product was approximately 6 percent.

Field crops (millet, sorghum, wheat, barley, and alfalfa), livestock, and dates are the principal agricultural products of Saudi Arabia. Production of livestock is rooted in the traditions of Bedouin life. Sheep, goats, and camels outnumber cattle by a margin of twenty to one. Livestock is associated with susbsistence farming and makes a relatively small contribution to commercial agriculture. Considerable beef is imported because domestic production of beef is low in relation to the size of the market for it.

From the viewpoint of development strategy, there are two important characteristics of the agricultural sector. First, while agriculture contributed only six percent of gross domestic product by 1971, it accounted for 40 percent of employment. Second, much of Saudi Arabian agricultural activity is associated with the nomadic life of the Bedouin. The nomadic sector makes only a small economic contribution.

Other Sectors. The trade and services sector, which includes banking, wholesale and retail trade, insurance, and real estate, accounted for approximately 10 percent of gross domestic product in 1971. Wholesale and retail trade accounted for more than half the value added in this category, and this sector grew at an annual average rate of about 10 percent in the period under consideration. Activity in trade was tied closely to the growth of imports and to improved facilities for transportation and communication in the kingdom.

Most banking and insurance services have been contracted outside the kingdom. Other service activities, such as those of restaurants, laundries, barber shops, and the few hotels, have tended to be provided by very small business enterprises.

Government Appropriations and Expenditures. Since 1960 the government sector has undergone a transformation in functions, in the level of its operations, and in administrative capabilities. In 1960 the Saudi Arabian government did not have a workable national budget and, before that, revenues were treated as the personal income of the king and the royal family. In this earlier period revenues were squandered in nonproductive activities. Indeed, the principal reason that King Faisal replaced his brother Saud was the financial position of the kingdom. The institution of a national budget and a reduction in the share of revenues going to the royal family established the basis for the sound fiscal position that prevailed during most of the 1960s. Budgets were balanced, and foreign debts that had been incurred during the 1950s were repaid.

The Saudi concept of a balanced budget is unconventional. It means not that current fiscal year expenditures equal current fiscal year receipts but, rather, that expenditures do not have to be financed by the issuance of government debt. Thus, when reserves are drawn down to finance current expenditures—or, conversely, when excess revenues are allocated to reserves—the budget is described as balanced.

Between 1960 and 1970, government revenues increased from $350.9 million to $1,385.8 million, but there were major variations in the rates of increase. After registering average annual increases of approximately 20 percent during the 1962–67 period, revenues declined in 1968, and in 1969 and 1970 they increased only 12 percent a year. Of course, the variations in government revenues made planned development difficult.

Saudi appropriations and expenditures during the 1960s can best be studied by categorizing them as consumption and development. Any categorization of Saudi expenditures must be somewhat arbitrary. The Saudi budget category of development expenditures includes some not typically labeled as such in other countries. Basically, the budget for development expenditures corresponds to a projects budget. Because the Saudi government includes all construction (including that of government buildings and mosques) in the projects budget, it is clear that the development category does not correspond to the common use of the term "development expenditures." All non-

21

project expenditures are labeled as consumption. Because expenditures are categorized in this manner in Saudi Arabian statistics and because it is impossible to obtain the detail that would allow separation of expenditures into subcategories, the proportions that are for consumption rather than for development tend to be understated.

From 1960 to 1970, appropriations for development increased more rapidly than did appropriations for consumption. Appropriations for consumption increased from $304 million in 1959 to $730 million in 1970; during the same period, development appropriations rose from $15 million to $590 million. Development appropriations as a percentage of total appropriations increased from 5 percent in 1959 to 20 percent in 1964 and to 45 percent in 1970.

Government expenditures increased more slowly than appropriations. Statistics on government expenditures before 1964 are not available. For the remainder of the 1960s, consumption expenditures kept pace with or even exceeded appropriations, but development expenditures lagged behind. In addition to administrative delays, there were delays in receiving bids, letting contracts, and implementing the contracts. During this period Saudi officials were anxious to avoid the experience of the 1950s, when the government was threatened with financial collapse.

By the late 1960s, the rate at which development projects were completed had improved, and by 1971 development expenditures were 88 percent of appropriations, whereas the ratio during the mid-1960s had averaged about 50 percent.[7]

Four major characteristics of the 1960–71 period are significant for an evaluation of the potential performance of the Saudi development effort. First, total expenditures approximated 90 percent of appropriations. Second, expenditures as a percentage of appropriations for development rose, averaging about 80 percent for the 1968–71 period. Third, expenditures for consumption kept pace with appropriations for this period. Finally, appropriations kept pace with revenues, indicating that the Saudis intended to spend their revenues even when they were increasing rapidly.[8]

The 1971–72 period provides an illustration of the last point. Appropriations were only about two-thirds of revenues in 1971. The reason is that estimated revenues were only $1,418 million, or $654 million less than realized revenues. It was the unexpected rise

[7] Donald A. Wells, *Saudi Arabian Revenues and Expenditures: The Potential for Foreign Exchange Savings* (Washington, D.C.: Resources for the Future, 1974), p. 10.

[8] Ibid., p. 11.

of revenues in 1971 that caused appropriations as a percentage of revenues to drop. The government reacted to the budgetary surplus by raising appropriations by 70 percent in 1972. Appropriations for development increased 94 percent, while appropriations for consumption increased 45 percent. The budget for 1972 was virtually balanced in spite of the doubling of revenues during 1971 and 1972. A slight budgetary surplus in 1972 did result when revenues again were underestimated somewhat.

Faisal Al-Bashir studied Saudi government spending during the 1960–70 period.[9] He concluded that for each fiscal year the level of both revenues and appropriations for consumption in the previous year were the principal determinants of consumption appropriations. Expenditure programs tended to be carried over from one year to the next, a condition of government spending not unique to Saudi Arabia. Revenues from the preceding year were the principal determinant in estimating current revenues, and appropriations tended to match changes in revenues. Al-Bashir concluded, on the basis of his analysis, that the government's long-run marginal propensity to consume, as measured by the relationship of appropriations for consumption to revenues, was 0.661 for the period from 1960 to 1970. Thus, approximately two-thirds of anticipated increases in revenues were appropriated for consumption.

The major conclusions to be drawn from an analysis of the 1960–71 period are these:

• Even during a period when revenues rose rapidly, total government appropriations tended to keep pace with revenues. Because of unexpected increases in revenues, appropriations for any one year might have lagged behind revenues, but appropriations were increased commensurately the following year.

• Appropriations for consumption expenditures increased steadily, averaging about 16 percent a year throughout the 1960–71 period.

• A principal reason that expenditures diverged from appropriations is that revenues fluctuated considerably during the period studied.

• Expenditures for development often lagged behind appropriations. Unspent development allocations were often transferred to other categories of the budget, particularly defense and other consumption expenditures.

---

[9] "An Econometric Model of the Saudi Arabian Economy: 1960-1970." Ph.D. dissertation, University of Arizona, 1973. Most of the budget figures for this period which are used in the present study were compiled by Al-Bashir.

- During the latter part of the period, development expenditures rose as a percentage of appropriations.

The experience of Saudi Arabia during the 1960s suggests that both the desire and the capability for increasing spending rapidly were present. Whenever revenues increased, rises in expenditures followed quickly, almost automatically. It does not follow that Saudi Arabia was always capable of spending its new level of revenues immediately. The experience does demonstrate that expenditures rose rapidly and that the gap between revenues and expenditures closed whenever the Saudis had had time to adjust to the new levels of income and wealth.

The First Five-Year Plan

Revenues. In the period following the Middle East War of 1967, Saudi government revenues increased relatively slowly. Beginning in 1971, however, revenues began to rise rapidly. Petroleum revenues rose through a combination of increased production, increases in the posted price, and increases in the tax rates on the income of the oil companies. As a result, for the years of the plan, 1971–75, the revenues of the government (calculated in riyals) increased 40 percent in each of the first two years, 38 percent in the third year, 168 percent in the fourth, and 138 percent in the final year. While the levels of the revenues will be higher under the five-year plan initiated in July 1975, Saudi Arabia has already experienced its highest rates of increase in revenues. Though it is, of course, natural to focus on the large increase in revenues that resulted, when the posted price of Saudi oil was raised from an average of $3.28 a barrel in 1973 to $10.46 a barrel in 1974, revenues were also rising rapidly during the 1971–73 period. By examining the government's expenditure policies during this period, we can determine the degree to which expenditures kept pace with revenues, the expenditure policies that emerged, and the effects of these on the Saudi economy.

Actual revenues increased rapidly during the period of the plan (see Table 1). Revenues were 71 percent higher in 1971 than in 1970. For 1972 and 1973, revenues increased an average of 40 percent each year, then jumped 168 percent in 1974. These revenues were considerably higher than had been anticipated when the plan was adopted in 1970, and the government found it necessary to revise its budgets and programs continuously upward. Even though Saudi authorities raised their estimates of revenues during this period as the trend emerged, estimated revenues were less than actual revenues

Table 1

GOVERNMENT REVENUES, APPROPRIATIONS AND EXPENDITURES, 1971–76 [a]

(billions of Saudi riyals)

Item	1971	1972	1973	1974	1975	1976
Estimated revenues	6.4	10.8	13.2	22.8	98.2	95.8
Actual revenues	7.9	11.1	15.4	41.3	101.4 [a]	n.a.
Appropriations	6.4	10.8	13.2	22.2	45.7	110.9
Actual expenditures [b]	5.8	7.3	9.2	16.5	30.3 [a]	n.a.

Notes: Appropriations, expenditures, and revenues are presented in riyals because these are the figures used as a basis for budget decisions in Saudi Arabia. The increase in terms of dollars would be greater because the riyal has appreciated in value 23 percent during this period, from 4.5 riyals to the dollar in 1971 to 3.47 riyals to the dollar in 1975.

Years correspond to the closest Saudi fiscal year.

[a] Estimates.

[b] Excludes aid to other Arab countries.

Source: Central Planning Organization, *Development Plan, 1975–1980*, and Saudi Arabian Monetary Agency [SAMA], *Annual Report 1975* (Riyadh), pp. 11-15.

each year. Estimated revenues were 81 percent of actual revenues in 1971, 97 percent in 1972, 86 percent in 1973, and 54 percent in 1974. In 1975, actual revenues exceeded estimated revenues by 3 percent.

Appropriations and Expenditures. For each of the years except 1975, budgeted appropriations were set equal to estimated revenues. In other words, even during a period when estimated revenues were increasing rapidly, Saudi authorities attempted to make use of all of their expected revenues. Only in 1975, when estimated revenues increased more than fourfold, were appropriations established at a level below estimated revenues. Even in 1975, when revenues were 101 billion riyals, appropriations were more than doubled, from 22.2 billion riyals to 45.7 billion riyals. From 1971 to 1975, the annual increase in appropriations averaged 66 percent.

Actual expenditures did not keep pace with appropriations. In each of the years since 1971, actual expenditures were less than appropriations. Actual expenditures were 67 percent of appropriations in 1972, 70 percent in 1973, 72 percent in 1974, and 66 percent in 1975.[10] During the 1972–75 period, when both estimated revenues

---

[10] SAMA, *Annual Report 1975*, pp. 13 and 157.

and actual revenues increased considerably, it would appear significant that actual expenditures increased at a rapid rate: 26 percent in 1972, 27 percent in 1973, 79 percent in 1974, and 83 percent in 1975.

There is one major omission from the data on actual expenditures, however—namely, foreign assistance to other countries. For example, Saudi Arabian commitments of bilateral aid were estimated to be over $2 billion in 1974.[11] Saudi Arabian aid to other Arab countries began in 1967, when after the Arab-Israeli war in June of that year, Saudi Arabia agreed to supply almost $200 million yearly to Syria, Jordan, and Egypt all together, according to the terms of the Khartoum agreement. This aid continued on a regular basis through 1973. When revenues increased to their much higher levels of 1974, new commitments of aid were made. In addition to a new $100 million grant to Egypt made in April 1974, Saudi Arabia announced a grant of $300 million to Egypt in August 1974 as part of a new $1.5 billion commitment. Aid has also been extended to a wide range of countries, including Niger, Somalia, Sudan, Uganda, the People's Democratic Republic of Yemen, Bahrain, Mauritania, Morocco, Tunisia, and Liberia. In addition to bilateral aid, Saudi Arabia has also pledged funds to the oil facility of the International Monetary Fund (IMF). Actual aid expenditures were $673 million in 1974 and $1,664 million in 1975. If we were to include aid expenditures, the rise in actual expenditures by Saudi Arabia has been greater than what is indicated in Table 1.

Development appropriations were 45 percent of total appropriations in 1970. For the 1971–74 period, development averaged 46 percent of total appropriations. With the very large increase in revenues in 1975, project appropriations dropped to 26 percent of total revenues but were 58 percent of total appropriations. For the period as a whole, given the large overall increase in revenues, it is remarkable that development appropriations have remained as high as they have. Expenditures for development have not kept pace with appropriations to the extent that expenditures for consumption have. Actual development expenditures were 72 percent of total appropriations in 1974 and estimated at 57 percent in 1975.[12]

From the figures in Table 2, the growth and importance of appropriations for national security become evident. Many of the grant and aid programs are associated with national security; defense expenditures, which had averaged only about 10 percent of total expenditures in the late 1960s and early 1970s, reached 21.6 percent of total

---

11 IMF Survey, November 18, 1974, p. 357.
12 SAMA, Annual Report 1975, p. 50.

Table 2

ANALYSIS OF GOVERNMENT APPROPRIATIONS (1975)

Item	Percent
Defense	21.6
Transportation and communications	13.1
Administration	12.7
Utilities and urban development	11.4
Education, vocational training and cultural affairs	9.1
Health and social affairs	4.6
Agriculture	1.3
Trade, industry and services	0.9
Special funds, grants, subsidies and aid programs	25.3

Source: Central Planning Organization, *Development Plan, 1975–1980*, p. 37.

expenditures in 1975. The ill-defined nature of national security makes it difficult to establish limits to expenditures for defense when revenues increase considerably and some remain unspent. There is some evidence that unspent development allocations in the past have been spent for national defense.

Economic Growth. As a result of the unprecedented growth in government revenues and expenditures, gross domestic product increased from 22.9 billion riyals in 1971 to an estimated 148.8 billion riyals in 1975. In dollars, per capita product for 1975 was between $7,000 and $8,000. Gross domestic product rose 112 percent between 1971 and 1975. In constant prices, the growth rate for gross domestic product was slightly more than 13 percent in 1970 and then at a compound annual rate of 20.5 percent from 1971 to 1973. Gross domestic product increased by 15 percent in 1974.

Real gross domestic product is derived by calculating domestic gross output and deflating this figure by implicit price deflators. Because petroleum prices have risen fourfold over a two-year period, real output is unrealistically deflated. When one adjusts real output for a terms-of-trade effect, recognizing that the increases in petroleum prices result in greater real national income because of the contribution of petroleum to greater import-purchasing power, the rate of increase for income for 1974 is seen to be much greater than 10 percent. If adjustment is made for the terms-of-trade effect, the average annual

Table 3

GROSS DOMESTIC PRODUCT: RELATIVE SHARES
(percentage)

Item	1971	1972	1973	1974	1975 [a]
Oil	62.3	66.1	70.3	84.0	86.6
Private, nonoil	29.8	26.4	23.7	13.1	11.0
Government	7.9	7.5	6.0	2.9	2.4

[a] Estimated.
Source: Central Planning Organization, *Development Plan, 1975–1980*, p. 24.

rate of growth of real national income between 1971 and 1974 is estimated at approximately 45 percent.[13]

Structure of the Economy. The Central Planning Organization of Saudi Arabia has calculated value added for various sectors of the economy for the 1971–75 period (Table 3). The spectacular growth of the petroleum sector increased its share of gross domestic product from 62 percent in 1971 to 86.6 percent in 1975. The share of the private, nonoil sector declined from 29.8 percent to 11.0 percent during the same period. The share of the government sector also declined in terms of value added.

Capital Formation. In real terms, fixed capital formation as a percentage of gross domestic product has averaged close to 18 percent throughout the 1971–75 period. This percentage is calculated after the value of gross domestic product has been adjusted downward to account for the rise in value resulting from the increased price of oil. Construction accounts for about three-fourths of total fixed capital formation and for about one-fourth of private nonoil output in the kingdom. It is the subsector in the private nonoil sector that has increased its share of gross domestic product significantly during the past five years; its share in 1970 was only 15 percent.

In 1974, the latest year for which data are available, the following were the shares of gross fixed capital formation: oil, 46 percent; government, 35 percent; and private nonoil, 19 percent. It is only in the petroleum sector that equipment and materials other than for construction constitute a larger share of fixed capital formation than

---

[13] Central Planning Organization, *Development Plan, 1975-1980*, p. 23.

does construction. For the total of all sectors, construction tends to average about one-third of total capital formation.

Labor Force. It is estimated that the Saudi labor force grew at an average annual rate of 3.8 percent between 1970 and 1975. In 1975 it was estimated that the participation rate for Saudi males was 45 percent and for Saudi women 1 percent. The proportion of the total Saudi population participating in the labor force rose slightly from 22.2 to 23.3 percent during the five-year period.[14]

Approximately 20–25 percent of the labor force is non-Saudi.[15] Imported labor can be conveniently divided into two categories. The first is unskilled workers, most of whom immigrate unofficially from surrounding areas such as Yemen. Most are employed as day laborers in construction or other hand-labor occupations. The second group consists of skilled and semiskilled workers, most from other Arabic-speaking countries but some from Europe, the United States, and Asia, primarily Pakistan. Many of those from the United States work in the petroleum sector. A survey in 1973 revealed that of the foreign workers entering the labor force in the private sector, Arabs from outside the Arabian Peninsula held the largest share of positions classified as skilled equipment operators, services, sales, and agricultural. Westerners dominated the technical and scientific sector and the management sector. Asians made up the largest share of office workers.[16]

The Saudis are heavily dependent on foreign workers in the more highly skilled occupations. Non-Saudis outnumber Saudis in the technical and subprofessional classification, and there are 7,400 Saudis classified as managers and officials, while there are 6,300 non-Saudis.[17] During the 1970–75 period as a whole, Saudi dependence on non-Saudis in the skilled categories tended to increase.

Because of a lack of statistics, there is no accurate measurement of wage rates. The Central Planning Organization states generally that "wages are rising rapidly, particularly in the private sector, owing to the extremely tight labor market."[18] Wages are rising more rapidly in the private sector than in the public sector. The two most recent salary increases for government employees were given in 1973 and 1975. The 1973 increase was 15 percent, and 1975 increases ranged

---

[14] Ibid., p. 7.
[15] Ibid., pp. 247-248.
[16] Ibid., p. 8.
[17] Ibid., pp. 247-248.
[18] Ibid., p. 244.

Table 4
PERCENTAGE RATES OF INFLATION, 1971–75

Item	1971	1972	1973	1974	1975[a]
Private sector					
Oil	25	5	24	162	47
Nonoil	1	3	10	14	14
Government sector	3	3	7	7	15
Total nonoil	2	3	10	12	15

[a] Estimated for the first half of the year.
Source: Central Planning Organization, *Development Plan, 1975–1980*, p. 18.

from 20 to 30 percent.[19] During this period, also, personal income taxes were abolished, and many persons have received promotions in rank. There is every indication that wages and salaries have risen rapidly. One result of the rapid rise in wages is an intensification of migration from rural areas to urban areas. In 1970, approximately 40 percent of the population was in rural areas, but by 1975 the proportion was only about 28 percent.[20]

Prices. Overall price indices are not very useful in analyzing price movements in Saudi Arabia. Petroleum represents 86 percent of gross domestic product. With the large increases in prices of petroleum, overall measures would give very high rates of inflation, which would have little meaning in an analysis of the Saudi economy inasmuch as almost all of the petroleum output is exported. An index of nonoil prices gives a better estimate. For nonoil sectors of the economy, prices have increased by about 50 percent during the period from 1971 to 1975 (Table 4). Most of that increase was in the last three years, with rates of inflation of 10 percent in 1973, 12 percent in 1974, and 15 percent in 1975 (based on estimates for the first half of the year). It appears the rate of inflation may have reached an annual rate of 50 percent by early 1976. The rate of inflation is highest on imported goods and on housing.

The government has taken a number of measures to reduce the impact of inflation. Taxes have been reduced or eliminated, subsidies were introduced for imports of milk, flour, rice, sugar, meats, vegetable oils and fats, and medicines, and electricity rates have been

---

[19] SAMA, *Annual Report 1975*, p. 10.
[20] *Development Plan, 1975-1980*, p. 579.

reduced through legislation and subsidies.[21] Because of these government measures, the lack of good statistics on prices, and the wide variations in consumption purchases among different income groups, little can be said with assurance about the effect of these price increases on the Saudis. For most, real incomes are likely to have increased considerably during this period.

Summary. During the 1970–75 period the Saudi economy showed unprecedented growth using a wide range of economic measures—gross domestic product, government revenues, government expenditures, and foreign assets. While there are troublesome problems emerging, such as rising prices and shortages of labor, most societies would choose to cope with the economic problems of Saudi Arabia in preference to their own. Because of the unprecedented increase and magnitude of revenues, the next decade will be a crucial one for Saudi Arabia in establishing the structure of economic activity in the kingdom and the basis for rising standards of living for the population. Saudi Arabia's policies will also be important for the rest of the world, given the importance of Saudi oil and the emergence of Saudi Arabia as a major capital exporter. In the next chapter, the development strategy proposed under the new five-year plan and the conditions and structure of the Saudi economy will be examined.

Before turning to the future, however, I should like to summarize what the Saudi authorities consider to be the highlights of development during the 1970–75 period.[22]

- There has been an extensive water exploration and water supply program. Seven desalination plants were put into operation.
- Agricultural production grew slowly.
- Petroleum production and prices were increased substantially. New gas-oil separation capacity, water-injection facilities, natural gas liquid processing plants, and supporting facilities were installed.
- Four licenses for the exploration and development of mineral resources were granted, and major exploration and mapping programs were initiated.
- Electrical capacity was expanded and electrical rates were reduced. A program to standardize service was begun.
- Expansion of manufacturing not based on hydrocarbons overfulfilled targets of the first plan, but manufacturing activities related to petroleum fell short of targets.

---

[21] SAMA, *Annual Report 1975*, pp. 12, 76.
[22] *Development Plan, 1975-1980*, pp. 46-52.

- Construction activity more than doubled over the five-year period.
- Education and health services grew very rapidly. In addition, information services through radio and television expanded rapidly.
- Social welfare programs were strengthened considerably.
- All major commercial and administrative centers are now connected with a network of roads and air service. Telecommunications services have not kept pace with the development of the economy. The postal service is inadequate.
- A program has begun for upgrading the physical appearance and amenities of municipalities.
- Housing construction has lagged behind demand.
- Valuable administrative experience has been achieved by government agencies and ministries.

These points are a blend of the aspirations, achievements, and shortcomings of the development process over the past five years. They condition the thinking of Saudi authorities and help to explain some of the emphases of the new five-year plan.

3
THE DEVELOPMENT PLAN, 1975-1980

Development Goals

The development goals of Saudi Arabia are stated in very broad terms. They are to

Maintain the religious and moral values of Islam.
Assure the defense and internal security of the Kingdom.
Maintain a high rate of economic growth by developing economic resources, maximizing earnings from oil over the long term, and conserving depletable resources.
Reduce economic dependence on export of crude oil.
Develop human resources by education, training, and raising standards of health.
Increase the well-being of all groups within the society and foster social stability under circumstances of rapid social change.
Develop the physical infrastructure to support achievement of the above goals.[1]

While goals related to Islam and to national defense are no less important than the other goals, there will be no attempt to include a discussion of their significance for economic development except in general terms. The development plan contains no details on the achievement of these two goals. Also, before examining the other stated goals in greater detail, it is interesting to note the ambiguous statement of the planning authorities on the role of the private sector in the development process:

The economic system of Saudi Arabia is based on the principles of free economy where a substantial part of the pro-

---

[1] Central Planning Organization, *Development Plan, 1975-1980*, p. 1.

duction and distribution of goods and services is left to individuals and groups enjoying freedom in their dealings and transactions. While the Government of Saudi Arabia will uphold the market system and encourage the private sector to play a fundamental role in the accelerated growth and development of the country, it will take all necessary measures to make the market system conform to the larger social interests of the country.[2]

There are three reasons for accepting the development plan's emphasis on the private sector. First, private enterprise and private property are consistent with the independence and freedom associated with Bedouin culture and traditions. It is unlikely that the Saudis would be comfortable with the regimentation and restraints that would follow direct government control over all economic activity. Second, the Saudi authorities recognize that they do not have the administrative capacity to direct all economic activity in the kingdom now, nor will they have it in the foreseeable future. Moreover, in an economy in which exports and imports are comparatively large, central control of the economy is less likely to be feasible than in one which is more nearly self-contained. Third, the Saudis have had a favorable experience in working with foreign firms, and they are confident of their abilities to integrate the operations of private firms into the economy in a manner consistent with government objectives and policies.

The last point deserves discussion. One of the experiences conditioning the attitudes of the Saudis toward private foreign companies is the experience of the Saudi Arabian government with Aramco. The importance of government revenues from Aramco has already been discussed. The political dominance of the Saud family has been closely tied to the income received from petroleum, and 90 percent of this income has come from Aramco. What disagreements there have been between Aramco and the Saudi government have been resolved for the most part by means of bilateral negotiations; the relinquishment of concession areas, the introduction of income taxes in 1952, the establishment of posted prices beginning in the early 1950s, the expensing of royalties, income from the Trans-Arabian pipeline (TAPLINE), and levels of production have been disputed at various times during the past forty years. The success of bilateral negotiations between Aramco and the Saudi government has resulted from the essentially conservative bargaining position of the govern-

---

[2] Ibid., p. 3.

ment and the acceptance by Aramco of the fact that changing political and economic circumstances have required revision of the agreement.

Major Elements of Development Strategy

There are three major elements of development strategy advanced by the plan.

First, there is strong emphasis on diversification of economic activity through increasing agricultural and industrial production. Diversification is advocated as the means of reducing dependence on production and export of crude oil in anticipation of the depleting of oil resources. There is a strong reliance on increasing industrial production that is based on natural gas and mineral resources. Agriculture is to be stimulated and subsidized by agricultural extension activities and credit and input subsidies.

Second, manpower programs aimed at increasing the productivity of labor are regarded as essential. During the period when Saudi manpower skills are being developed, non-Saudi laborers are to be imported in large numbers. The estimated increase in non-Saudi laborers during the period of the plan is 499,000, a significant increase from the estimated non-Saudi labor force of 314,000 in 1975.

Third, a plan has been developed for distributing the growth in economic activity among five regions. Industrial bases are to be centered in the eastern and western regions along the coasts of the kingdom. The region around Riyadh is to be developed as an administrative center with light industry. Agricultural and mineral development will be pushed in the northern and southwestern regions.

Having observed the outline of the master plan, with its emphasis on industrialization, we can examine more closely the policies and programs associated with each of the major goals.

High Rate of Economic Growth. The five-year plan is ambitious. It anticipates an annual growth rate in gross domestic product of 10.2 percent in real terms. Most sectors of the economy will share in this growth. Only agriculture, at 4 percent a year, petroleum refining at 5 percent, and ownership of dwellings at 6 percent are expected to grow at less than the average rate. Most segments of the public sector, including education, public health, and defense, will average close to 15 percent. The private nonoil sector is expected to grow at an annual rate of 13.4 percent, and the government sector at 13.3 percent. The oil sector is projected to grow at an annual rate of 9.7 percent.

Table 5

RELATIVE SECTORAL SHARES OF GROSS DOMESTIC
PRODUCT, 1975 AND 1980

Sector	GDP in Current Prices (billions of riyals)		Relative Shares (percent)	
	1975	1980	1975	1980
Oil	128.7	261.3	86.6	82.1
Private nonoil	16.4	47.5	11.0	14.9
Government	3.6	9.6	2.4	3.0
Total	148.7	318.4	100.0	100.0

Source: Central Planning Organization, *Development Plan, 1975–1980*, p. 78.

There is little change in the structure of the economy anticipated for the near term (Table 5). The share of the oil sector will decline only from 86.6 percent in 1975 to 82.1 percent in 1980. Hidden within the overall increase in the share of the private nonoil sector from 11.0 percent to 14.9 percent is a decline in the relative importance of agriculture and an increase in the relative importance of construction. Construction is estimated to represent one-third of the total value added in the private nonoil sector.

Because of world inflation and the rapid growth of demand in Saudi Arabia, prices are expected to increase 15 percent a year on average. The highest rates of inflation are anticipated for those sectors that are expected to grow the most rapidly in real terms: construction, mining and quarrying, utilities, transportation and communication, trade, and business services.

The high projected rates of economic growth require an extraordinary investment program. Construction projects planned for the 1975–80 period total 258 billion riyals, or $74.4 billion (at the 1975 exchange rate of 3.47 riyals to the dollar). Other investment projects might add another $12 billion to these requirements, bringing the total to about $86.5 billion. To appreciate the magnitudes involved, we should note that if construction in Saudi Arabia were to increase at a compound annual rate of 25 percent, the cumulative total of the value of construction by 1980 would be $37.5 billion. In relation to existing plant and equipment, the capital requirements of the development plan are unprecedented.

Reduction of Economic Dependence on Crude Oil. The plan is candid in its assessment of the role of the petroleum sector:

The above projections do not indicate any near-term change in the basic structure of the Kingdom's economy. The importance of oil is over-riding and will continue into the foreseeable future. Domestically-based, energy-intensive industries will further enhance oil's role in the economy. The long-term objective of diversification of the sources of national income and reduced dependence on oil is, therefore, somewhat paradoxical, because oil revenues are the means through which the Government finances the Kingdom's economic and social development programs—the principal means to diversification.

Thus, the speed with which diversification can be pursued is dependent on the extent and rapidity the Government achieves in exploiting its oil resources. The more successful the exploitation, the larger oil's share of GDP. The important criterion to use in assessing the economy's diversification efforts over the next several years is not oil's share of GDP, but whether or not consistent real growth is taking place in the other sectors.[3]

According to the plan, the higher rates of growth of the non-oil private sector are the measure of diversification. The plan reflects a recognition that little can be accomplished to reduce the dominance of the petroleum sector in a five-year period. The dependence on petroleum in the near term must also be recognized in any assessment of the appropriate rate of exploitation of oil resources, in which the pressures for conserving petroleum reserves must be taken into account.

While it is recognized that little can be done to reduce Saudi dependence upon the oil sector during the next five years, the plan does include an attempt to begin a process that might have that effect in the long run. The plan puts heavy emphasis on industrialization and on promoting the manufacture of a wide range of products. Many measures have been initiated or proposed for the encouragement of private investment in manufacturing.

The industrial sector is approached in the plan by way of a distinction between industries that are based on hydrocarbons and those that are not. The principal reason for the distinction is jurisdictional. Petromin is responsible for the larger projects in manufacturing that utilize hydrocarbon resources. The Ministry of Commerce and Industry and the Industrial Studies and Development Center together are to administer programs involving other manufacturing ventures. The association of hydrocarbon ventures with

---

[3] Ibid., p. 79.

Petromin means that government participation in this subsector of industry will be greater than in the nonhydrocarbon subsector.

For the Petromin-administered hydrocarbon subsector, the over-all program includes:

• New refineries and the expansion of existing refineries for both domestic consumption and export.

• The establishment of facilities for gathering and treating gas in the eastern oil-producing region and the construction of petroleum and gas pipelines to the major urban centers in the central and western regions.

• The establishment of facilities for manufacturing petrochemicals, fertilizers, and steel and aluminum.

Major projects are to be started that will utilize petroleum and gas as raw materials and as sources of energy in implementing the overall program. The most important projects, statistics of which are summarized in Table 6, include the following:

• Facilities costing $4.6 billion for gathering and treating gas in the eastern region as the first stage of the development of new hydrocarbon-based industries. The facilities will provide 1.6 billion cubic feet of gas a day for industrial use.

• The construction of four petrochemical complexes, three in the eastern region and one in the west. Once installed, these plants will produce 2 million tons of ethylene a year.

• Three export refineries with a total investment of $1.9 billion. Each is to have a capacity of 250,000 barrels a day.

• The construction of a lubricating oil refinery in the eastern region with a capacity of 12,000 barrels of lubricating oil stock a day and 95,000 barrels of low-sulphur oil a day.

• The construction of a 3.5 million-ton steel facility in the eastern region for a total investment of $1.6 billion and of an aluminum facility to cost $400 million. The steel mill is to produce metal pellets, basic shapes and bar, and pipes. In addition to the building of these two facilities, a feasibility study for a major new rolling mill for reinforcing bars is to be completed in 1976.

• Two fertilizer plants in the eastern region, with a combined annual capacity of 220,000 tons of ammonia and 800,000 tons of urea, will be constructed at a cost of $400 million.

• For a total of $1.8 billion, the construction of a crude-oil line from the east coast to the west coast with a capacity of 2.4 million barrels a day and a liquefied natural gas line, also crossing the country, with a capacity of 356,000 barrels a day.

Table 6
MAJOR DEVELOPMENT PROGRAMS FOR HYDROCARBON-BASED INDUSTRIES, 1975–85

Program or Project	Investment (billions of dollars)	Capacity	Peak Employment (number of workers)
Eastern region			
Gas gathering and treatment	4.6	1,600 million cu.ft/day	2,300
Petrochemical complexes (4, of which 3 to be initiated, 1975–80)	2.6	2.0 million tons/year ethylene	6,800
Export refineries (2)	1.3	500 thousand bbl/day	1,700
Lubricating oil refinery	0.6	107 thousand bbl/day [a]	550
Fertilizer plants (4, of which 2 to be initiated, 1975–80)	0.4	2 million tons/year	2,000
Aluminum plant	0.4	210 thousand tons/year	1,900
Steel plant	1.6	3.5 million tons/year	8,600
Subtotal	11.5		23,850
Western region			
Crude line to west	1.5	2.4 million bbl/day ⎫	550
NGL line to west	0.3	356 thousand bbl/day ⎬	
Export refinery	0.6	250 thousand bbl/day ⎭	850
Petrochemical complex	0.7	500 thousand ton/year ethylene	1,700
Subtotal	3.1		3,100
Total	14.6		26,950

a 12,000 barrels a day of lubricating oil stock, 95,000 barrels a day of low-sulphur oil.
Source: Central Planning Organization, *Development Plan, 1975–1980*, p. 202.

These major projects represent a total investment of $14.6 billion. Some are scheduled to be completed as late as 1983, but most are planned for completion by 1981. When all are in full operation it is estimated that they will provide employment for a total of almost 27,000 workers as compared with an estimated 46,500 workers who were employed in manufacturing in 1975. It is recognized in the plan, however, that perhaps not all of the proposed projects will be initiated and completed during the period covered by the plan. In the schedule of finance for the investment in hydrocarbons, "scheduled investment assumes that 60 percent of total investments in projects to be initiated during the Plan . . . will actually be made during the Plan." [4]

For manufacturing activities other than in hydrocarbons, the participation of the government is less direct. The government has initiated programs to provide incentives for private firms, both domestic and foreign. These include equity capital and loans, organizational assistance, feasibility studies, assistance with operations, tariff exemptions on imported materials and equipment, tax incentives, procurement preferences, protective tariffs, sites for industrial estates, subsidies for the training of Saudi manpower, and export assistance.[5]

The major planned developments in industries not based on hydrocarbons include: [6]

- Tenfold expansion of cement production.
- The construction of plants to provide agricultural inputs and to process agricultural outputs (including flour milling and sugar refining).
- The promotion of a wide range of manufacturing activities, including construction materials and household and commercial equipment.

Development of Human Resources. Major changes in the quantity and quality of the labor force are anticipated in the plan. The overall annual rate of growth of the labor force is projected at 7.8 percent (see Table 7).

The number of Saudis in the labor force is expected to increase at the rate of 3.4 percent a year; the increase will result from the combination of a higher population and a greater rate of participation by both men and women. The spectacular growth in the labor force, however, is expected to come about through the importation of labor. The non-Saudi labor force, numbering 314,000 in 1975, is expected

---

[4] Ibid., p. 215.

[5] Ibid., p. 188.

[6] Ibid., p. 194.

Table 7

COMPOSITION OF LABOR FORCE IN 1975 AND 1980

Category of Workers	Number of Workers (thousands)		Annual Rate of Growth (percent)
	1975	1980	1975–1980
Saudi men	1,259	1,470	3.1
Non-Saudi men	306	768	20.2
Subtotal	1,565	2,238	7.4
Saudi women	27	48	15.1
Non-Saudi women	8	45	41.2
Subtotal	35	93	21.6
Subtotal Saudi	1,286	1,518	3.4
Subtotal non-Saudi	314	813	21.0
Total	1,600	2,331	7.8

Source: Central Planning Organization, *Development Plan, 1975–1980*, p. 60.

to reach 813,000 by 1980. The projected average annual growth rate of non-Saudi labor is 21 percent. The reliance upon non-Saudi labor in the period of the plan is considerable: more than one-third of the labor force will be non-Saudi by 1980.

The largest increases are anticipated in the professional and technical group—142 percent—and the clerical group—124 percent. Except farmers and fishermen, all other groups (administrative and managerial, sales, service, and production) will increase also. The proportion of the labor force represented by farmers and fishermen is expected to decline from 27 percent in 1975 to 16 percent in 1980.

A maximum effort is to be directed at upgrading the skills and educational level of the Saudis. Within the government, various training programs, primarily under the direction of the Institute of Public Administration, are planned as an attempt to improve the skills of government employees. Elementary-school enrollment of boys is expected to increase from 401,000 in 1975 to about 677,000 in 1980, and of girls from 215,000 in 1975 to 353,000 in 1980. Similar increases are anticipated at the secondary and higher educational levels. Continuing education and vocational training programs are also to be expanded. Implementation of the plan will require 13,000 additional elementary teachers and 1,500 secondary-school teachers; the teaching staffs of all primary and secondary schools are expected to increase from 20,000 in 1975 to 51,000 in 1980.

Economic and Social Well-being. The roles of government and the individual in achieving economic and social well-being are delineated in the plan. "Social services will be developed to ensure that every group and individual, however disadvantaged, enjoys an adequate, dignified minimum standard of living; levels above this minimum will continue to be the reward of individual effort and achievement." [7]

The minimum standard of living is not defined. Social programs consist of subsidized health care and education, social security programs, community development, rehabilitation programs, youth programs, and services for the Bedouin. At present social security provides, without the recipients' having contributed to the program, pensions to persons more than sixty years old, to the partially or completely disabled, to orphans, and to women without support.

Development of the Physical Infrastructure. The established programs in transportation, communications, municipalities, and housing will be continued and accelerated. The first two have been the important elements of government development programs throughout the past decade. In the past few years more attention has been directed toward the requirements of municipalities and housing. Municipalities, which are settled places designated as municipalities by the government, have no independent sources of income and are dependent upon the national government for all their requirements.

With respect to transportation, the intention is to connect the major centers of population and to expand port facilities. More than 8,000 miles of paved roads and 6,200 miles of rural roads are to be constructed during the period of the plan. Port facilities at Jeddah, on the west coast, and Dammam, on the east coast, are to be enlarged in an attempt to increase fourfold the amount of tonnage that was handled in 1973. Mechanization of the handling of cargo is to be undertaken in an effort to improve the efficiency of port operations.

An extensive upgrading of telecommunications is to be attempted. At the end of 1974 there were not quite 94,000 telephone lines in the kingdom; the plan calls for the installation of 490,000 lines. The goal is to provide twenty telephones per hundred inhabitants of the larger cities and five telephones per hundred inhabitants of the smaller cities.

Until 1970, municipalities received relatively little attention in the allocation of governmental resources. Some progress was made during the next five years in dealing with the problems of municipalities. The number of settled places designated as municipalities rose

---

[7] Ibid., p. 2.

Table 8
PLANNED CONSTRUCTION OF HOUSES, 1976–80
(thousands of units)

Item	1976	1977	1978	1979	1980	Total
Private sector	20.3	21.9	24.0	26.5	29.4	122.1
Public sector	1.3	1.3	5.0	15.0	30.0	52.5
Project housing (temporary)	1.0	5.0	10.0	15.0	20.0	51.0
Total	22.5	28.2	39.0	56.5	79.4	225.6

Source: Central Planning Organization, *Development Plan, 1975–1980*, p. 582.

from fifty-four to eighty-five. Physical improvements were concentrated in roads, sewage, and drainage projects. Facilities such as public parks and public toilets were also installed. Despite these efforts, however, it is acknowledged that upgrading these types of facilities remains a substantial task. One of the problems is to recruit officials and construction contractors who are willing to work and to live in municipalities in remote areas. The financial requirements for an expected 162 municipalities by 1980 are more than $15 billion for the period, and this figure does not include expenditures for municipal water projects.

Housing has been a neglected sector of the economy. Private financial markets for housing are virtually nonexistent. With the pressures put on the construction industry by the overall development effort, the costs of labor and materials have risen considerably. Prices of residential land have increased even more rapidly than costs of labor and materials; in some places land values have increased tenfold. As a result, during the 1970–75 period, "as the direct by-product of rapid urban growth, and the shortages or rising costs of labor, land, and materials for residential buildings, housing in the Kingdom's cities has generally grown worse." [8] Approximately 75,000 standard or above-standard residential units were constructed between 1970 and 1975.

The plan calls for 225,000 housing units to be built during the 1976–80 period (see Table 8). The private sector is expected to maintain its predominant place in providing housing during the first four years of the plan. It is anticipated that time will be required for the public sector to become organized to complete its housing

[8] Ibid., p. 577.

projects, but by 1980 the public and private sectors should be sharing the market for the construction of residences on a fifty-fifty basis. Most public-sector housing will be prefabricated housing provided by foreign construction firms.

A major emphasis of the housing plan is "to ensure that enough housing, both permanent and temporary, is built during the plan period to accommodate the additional manpower needed to implement the Plan." [9] As part of this program, contractors on major development projects will be required to construct the temporary housing needed by the laborers working on these projects. Foreign laborers, especially, will require new temporary housing. The plan calls for 51,000 units to be built for this purpose during the five-year period.

The government will take major steps to help finance housing in the private sector. By 1980 a government agency, the Real Estate Development Fund, will be financing 50 percent of the private-sector housing. Loans to low- and moderate-income families will be subsidized; borrowers with higher incomes will receive funds through banks and other commercial channels. The total of government funds to be provided for housing is estimated at $4.1 billion. Total spending on housing will be considerably higher, of course.[10]

The Overall Magnitudes

It is obvious from the listings and descriptions of policies, programs, and projects that an acceleration of economic activity of great magnitude will be attempted throughout the period of the plan. The attempt is unprecedented for a country with such a small population and at such an early stage of its development.

Financial Requirements. The extent of the effort associated with the goals that have been adopted can be appreciated through an examination of the financial requirements of the plan.

A comparison of the first and second five-year plans—for 1970–75 and 1975–80, respectively—shows a ninefold increase in the estimated financial requirements (see Table 9). Total expenditures increase approximately nine times from the $16.1 billion spent during the first plan period to the $143.6 billion to be spent during the second. The largest increases are in the categories of development

---

[9] Ibid., p. 580.

[10] Estimated cost per unit (including land, land development, and building construction) is $47,800 for private-sector housing and $40,300 for public-sector housing.

Table 9

ESTIMATED FINANCIAL REQUIREMENTS,
1970–75 AND 1975–80
(billions of dollars)

Category	1970–75 Amount [a]	1970–75 Percent	1975–80 Amount [a]	1975–80 Percent
Development				
Economic resources	1.7	10.7	26.6	18.5
Human resources	2.9	18.1	23.1	16.1
Social	.7	4.4	9.6	6.7
Physical infrastructures	4.1	25.1	32.5	22.7
Subtotal development	9.4	58.3	91.8	63.9
Other				
Administration	3.0	18.6	11.0	7.7
Defense	3.7	23.1	22.5	15.7
External assistance, emergency funds, food subsidies, and general reserve	...	...	18.3	12.7
Subtotal, other	6.7	41.7	51.8	36.1
Total	16.1	100.0	143.6	100.0

[a] 1970–75 values have been adjusted to 1975 prices. Except for a few long-term projects, 1975–80 values are in 1975 prices.
Source: Central Planning Organization, *Development Plan, 1975–1980*, p. 600.

of economic resources and social development. The relative size of these increases is explained primarily by the low bases from which the increases are calculated for the 1970–75 period. In the total value of expenditures during the new plan period, development of physical infrastructures ranks highest ($32.5 billion); next is development of economic resources ($26.6 billion); third is development of human resources ($23.1 billion); and fourth is defense ($22.5 billion).[11] The four development sectors account for $91.8 billion, or 64 percent of total estimated expenditures.

Out of total expenditures of $143.6 billion, project expenditures, which are expenditures for undertakings with a completion date, account for $95.5 billion. Of that $95.5 billion, $68.9 billion is to go for projects categorized as development. Recurrent expenditures amount to $48.1 billion.

---

[11] Defense spending has been *assumed* to increase 20 percent a year.

The $143.6 billion represents only a partial accounting of investment and other expenditures affecting development in Saudi Arabia. The plan mentions five major categories of investment that it does not include:

> Investment by the private sector in agricultural development apart from that financed by agricultural credit.

> Investment by the oil companies in expanding oil production capacity.

> Investment by the private sector and joint-venture partners in industry, apart from the amounts to be financed by industrial credit.

> Investment by the private sector in commerce, transportation, and services.

> Investment in private-sector housing not financed by the Real Estate Development Fund.

To the extent that the private sector flourishes during the plan period, the extent of the claim on resources is understated in the plan.

Implementation of the Plan

As part of the resolution of the Council of Ministers, by whom the five-year development plan was adopted, procedures were established for implementation of the plan. This was a significant step in the planning process, inasmuch as under the previous plan there had been little formal commitment to implementation. The major provisions were that:

> All ministries and independent agencies shall comply with the contents of the Plan in preparing their annual budgets to achieve the targets set therein.

> The Budget Department of the Ministry of Finance and National Economy shall each year allocate the required funds for the projects and programs included in the Plan through optimum cooperation and coordination with a joint committee to consist of the Deputy Minister of Finance and Budget Affairs, the Vice President of the Central Planning Organization, and the Deputy Minister of the concerned ministry or independent agency.

> In case of disagreement, the matter will be settled by a decision taken by the Minister of Finance and National Economy, the Minister of State and President of the Central Planning Organization, and the Minister or agency head concerned.

Table 10

ANALYSIS OF EXPENDITURES FOR MAJOR DEVELOPMENT PROGRAMS, 1975–80

(billions of dollars)

Program	Amount
Water and desalination	9.8
Agriculture (excluding regional development)	1.4
Electricity	1.8
Manufacturing and minerals	13.0
Education	21.4
Health	5.0
Social programs and youth welfare	4.2
Roads, ports, and railroads	6.1
Civil aviation and Saudia Airline	4.3
Telecommunications and postal services	1.2
Municipalities	15.4
Housing	4.1
Holy cities and the pilgrimage	1.4
Other development	2.7
Subtotal, development	91.8
Defense	15.7
General administration	11.0
Funds	18.3
Subtotal, other	51.8
Total plan	143.6

Source: Central Planning Organization, *Development Plan, 1975–1980*, p. 602.

The Minister of State and President of the Central Planning Organization, the Minister of State for Financial Affairs and National Economy, the President of the Control and Investigation Organization, and the Chairman of the Advisors Section at the Council of Ministers shall formulate a follow-up system for plan implementation to be considered by the Council of Ministers.

All ministries, departments, and independent and semi-independent government corporations shall conduct the studies for programs and projects that fall within their jurisdiction of the Plan and the Central Planning Organization shall conduct such studies should those agencies fail to do so as scheduled in the Plan.[12]

---

[12] *Development Plan, 1975-1980*, pp. i-ii.

The major point of these provisions is to give greater authority to the Central Planning Organization in the planning and execution of government expenditures and policy. They signal, also, the fact that the government is concerned about compliance with the plan and the rate at which it is implemented.

Caveat

The development plan is 663 pages long. This brief summary of it is only an attempt to highlight those portions that help to understand the key elements of development strategy. Much detail has been omitted. Also, in the plan there is considerable attention given to administrative reorganization and to the plans made for improving administrative efficiency. These are essential to the successful development of the economy, and the fact that they are not treated here is not intended to minimize their importance. The strategy of development can, however, be understood without going into the details of these efforts.

4
AN EVALUATION OF
THE DEVELOPMENT PLAN

Introduction

The plan is a useful document for analytical purposes. Not only does it present data on the Saudi economy that are not available elsewhere, it also provides a good analysis of past economic performance and of interrelationships among the various sectors of the economy. A part of the new development plan is an accelerated program to generate and process the types and amounts of data that are necessary for effective decision making. In the present plan, even something so essential as a complete and reliable census was not available to the authorities.[1] At least part of the value of the plan to the Saudi authorities lies in the fact that it has given occasion for the gathering and organizing of a great many data that were necessary for its preparation.

From the viewpoint of assessing development strategy, it is important to determine the stature of the plan both for its political value and for its significance for development policy. At one extreme the plan could be the primary determinant for budget decisions; at the other, it might be an ineffectual statement of intentions, ignored in the budget decision-making process. Only after establishing what the plan is, and what it is not, can we make judgments about development strategy.

The approval of the objectives, programs, and projects of the plan by the Council of Ministers in its resolution of May 21, 1975, sanctions the principal elements of the plan and the planning process itself. The approval was accompanied by instructions to the ministries

---

[1] A census was completed in 1974 but the results had not been processed by the time the plan was completed and approved.

and agencies for compliance through the budget-making process. Earlier, the annual budgets of individual ministries had been prepared without direct reference to the development plan, and budget approvals were primarily the concern of the Ministry of Finance and National Economy. Now either the President or Vice-President of the Central Planning Organization has decision-making authority in allocating funds for projects and programs included in the plan and for ensuring the implementation of the plan.

In the personalized process of decision making within the Saudi government, the increased role for planning authorities reflects the growing personal political influence of Hisham Mohiddin Nazer, who previously was the Minister of State and President of the Central Planning Organization and who recently was designated Minister of Planning when the Central Planning Organization was given ministry status in 1975. Before the appointment of Nazer to these offices, the Central Planning Organization was headed by an adviser on foreign affairs to King Faisal and who played little active role in the Central Planning Organization. Under the leadership of Hisham Nazer, however, the Central Planning Organization had developed an independent status similar to that enjoyed by the ministries. The changing fortunes of the Central Planning Organization could be seen when, "In an unusual gesture of support for an individual minister, [Crown] Prince Fahd visited the planning organization and promptly endorsed its industrialization programme."[2] In the labyrinth of Saudi family politics, such a visit is significant. Such actions make it clear that it is important for the individual ministries to comply with the plan.

This heightened stature of both the plan and the newly designated Ministry of Planning is somewhat offset by the nature of the planning process in Saudi Arabia. Each ministry draws up its own set of objectives, programs, and projects. These separately determined ministry proposals are then incorporated in the overall development plan. There is considerable consultation between the individual ministries and agencies and the Ministry of Planning, the latter attempting to coordinate programs and to avoid duplication of activities and functions. Similarly, ministries and agencies consult among themselves when coordination is desirable or when jurisdictional problems appear. But these actions are subsidiary to the initiating role of the ministries themselves. Each individual ministry has its own political base; it is difficult for outside agencies or organizations to thwart its intentions

---

2. "Survey," *The Economist*, April 26, 1975, p. 67.

when it functions (and makes proposals) within its accepted jurisdiction.

Moreover, the power of the individual ministries is augmented when there is no effective budgetary constraint. When the national budget is tight, individual ministries must contend for funds within the Council of Ministers and in dealings with the Ministry of Finance, which has overall authority over budgetary allocations. But when the principal problem seems to be conceiving a sufficient number of projects and programs to use the vast sums available to the government, then the competitive constraint among ministries is lost and there is not much to replace it. For this reason, then, the plan has a built-in "shopping-list" bias. It becomes the task of the Planning Ministry to organize the requests of the ministries, organizations, and agencies and to sum them up. The development strategy as a whole tends to emerge from the sum of the parts rather than from the strategy determining the composition of programs and projects.

It is prudent to recognize that not all ministries are equal. Tribal and family loyalties abound throughout the government, and power and influence are closely tied to such relationships. For the planning process, the identification of centers of power is essential, for the planners must respond to these influences and accept the decisions that come from them.

These considerations help to explain why two important sectors (defense and petroleum) are not integral parts of the plan. Each receives nominal treatment in the plan, and the impression is that decision making in both sectors is separate from the degree of influence exerted by the plan and the Ministry of Planning in the rest of the economy.

It is assumed in the plan that defense spending will increase 20 percent a year. There is no indication of the way in which that rate of increase was arrived at; it is likely that the projected increases of defense expenditures are lower than the actual increases will be. Two major purchases indicate how quickly defense spending can rise. In 1973, published defense appropriations were approximately $900 million, or 27 percent of the national budget.[3] In December 1974, Saudi Arabia concluded an arms-purchase agreement with France. The $860 million package included about 200 tanks, 250 armored cars, and a surface-to-air missile system. One month later, in January 1975, Saudi Arabia contracted to purchase several squadrons (approximately 60 planes) of jet fighter planes, primarily including the Northrop F-5E Tiger jet, for $756 million. The level of defense spending initi-

---

[3] *The Economist*, May 5, 1973, p. 43.

ated at that time has led to an estimate that military expenditures of Saudi Arabia for 1975 were approximately $3 billion.[4] Because of the nonrecurrent nature of purchases of military hardware (barring a war), however, it is difficult to estimate total military expenditures for the next five years. For example, in another study it is estimated that the annual expenditure on arms will be $1 billion through 1980.[5]

It is thus difficult to anticipate the rate of increase of defense spending. What is likely is that defense spending will be determined outside the plan. While one cannot foresee financial constraints on other nondefense projects and programs as a result of defense spending, it is possible that defense spending might cause problems in the utilization of a particular product—cement, for example. Similarly, in a particular geographical region, defense requirements could preempt the use of housing, transportation, and communication facilities. It is doubtful that the existence of the plan will alter the priorities of the Ministry of Defense in any significant way.

The Ministry of Petroleum does not seem to be integrated into the development plan. Petroleum programs and projects are primarily characterized as studies and training. No discussion of production and pricing decisions which might have significance for the plan is included. In sum, there is no integration of the crude-oil sector as a producing sector in the development plan.

There are two reasons that the activities of the Ministry of Petroleum are not presented in detail in the plan. First, the Ministry of Petroleum has guarded its independence of the Central Planning Organization: it is unlikely to subject its activities to close supervision by the planning authorities. Second, decisions concerning pricing, production, and exploration in the oil sector are politically sensitive; given Saudi participation in OPEC, Saudi Arabia would not find it prudent or even possible to broadcast its intentions in this sector. In the absence of details of the crude oil sector, the development plan is left with a gap in its projections of projects and programs.

In estimating the resource and financial requirements of the next five years, there remains one major problem in formulating an effective plan. The private sector has not been adequately integrated into the planning process. As long as Saudi Arabia permits the private sector to play an important role in manufacturing, trade, and agriculture,

---

[4] DRI (Data Resources Institute) Energy Outlook, August 1975, Table 40, p. 112.
[5] Christopher A. Gebelein (economist, Shell Oil Co.), "Effects of Conservation on Oil Prices: Analysis of Misconceptions." Unpublished paper, revised, June 1975, p. 19.

then in the absence of better information about the private sector, the plan will be deficient. Thus, the development plan provides much information about the level and direction of public expenditures, but it contains very few reliable projections concerning the private sector. These appear to be the major elements of the economy that are not treated adequately in the plan. They may weaken the planning process by creating uncertainty, but there is little that the planning authorities can do to remedy the situation. Similarly, an assessment of development strategy can recognize their potential influences but must concentrate on those features of the plan that explain this strategy best.

Saudi Development Strategy

Six major features of development strategy emerge from a study of the Saudi development plan:

(1) There is a commitment to accelerated and early economic growth at a pace limited only by the kingdom's capacity to organize and to implement its programs and policies.

(2) The development of infrastructure is to continue to receive heavy emphasis.

(3) Industrialization is to be pushed to the utmost.

(4) Social welfare programs and some segments of consumption are to be subsidized by the government.

(5) There is to be a heavy reliance on imported labor.

(6) The private sector is to be encouraged and is expected to grow in spite of the preponderant influence of government revenues, expenditures, and policies.

Each of these features is an integral part of the overall strategy. Each tends to be an inevitable consequence of the others, and all are consistent with long-standing features of Saudi development policy. The emphasis on rapid economic growth and the subsidization of consumption are especially important.

Rapid Economic Growth. Soon after Saudi petroleum revenues had risen to their new levels, some observers suggested that the Saudis would or should limit their revenues and contain the growth process. It was suggested that the Saudis would want to limit the impact on their traditions and culture; Prince Saud el Faisal, son of the former king and deputy petroleum minister, expressed concern about "how much we can produce without harming ourselves." [6]

---

[6] *The Economist*, May 5, 1973, p. 42.

The planners rejected an approach that would limit expenditures with its consequent lowering of the rate of economic growth. Instead, the Saudis have adopted policies that will feature high rates of investment in both human and physical capital with the aim of providing rapidly rising levels of living and introducing a large number of new industries and enterprises into the kingdom.

A number of factors contributed to this decision. On the economic side, Saudi authorities seem to have concluded that the sudden burst in revenues has provided an opportunity that may not be sustained beyond an eight-to-ten-year period. The Saudi authorities realize that the high prices brought about by the OPEC cartel have triggered a worldwide response in exploration and production; they may fear that revenues may level off or even decline in real terms in the period beyond 1980. The opportunities for investment created by the enormous jump in revenues may be limited in time, existing only until revenues level off and expenditures increase. Domestic pressures may cause consumption expenditures to increase quickly, and the allocation of revenues to investment may be more difficult to achieve a few years from now than it is at present. In contemplating reduced revenues from the sale of crude oil, Saudi Arabia also has a special interest in diversifying its sources of production and income and reducing its dependence on the production and sale of crude oil. In view of the amount of time required to plan and execute major development projects, it would be desirable to initiate them as soon as possible in order to have as many as possible in place by 1980.

Another economic reason for initiating a major development program early is inflation. Development projects, like any other projects requiring a long time for completion, are subject to cost overruns. If one estimates worldwide rates of inflation at 5–8 percent during the next decade, the costs of development projects, given Saudi Arabia's dependence on imports of capital goods, could be reduced by initiating and completing them as soon as possible.

There are important political considerations as well that suggest that the Saudi authorities might be well advised to initiate projects as soon as possible. The pressures from other less developed countries, especially Arab and Moslem countries, to share the wealth of Saudi Arabia will be greater when revenues are accumulated as "surplus" than when they are spent. Another reason for increasing expenditures arises from political pressures within OPEC itself. To the extent that higher prices can be maintained in the future only by restricting production, some of the major producers, such as Iran and Venezuela, will argue for a criterion of "need." If revenues were accumulating, Saudi Arabia would feel increased pressures to restrict or reduce production in order to maintain the cartel price: one way to mitigate these pressures is to increase expenditures rapidly. Finally, there will be internal political pressures to share the wealth. The political leaders want to demonstrate their ability to use their new resources productively and also to provide increased employment and higher living standards for the people. All these considerations suggest that it is desirable from the viewpoint of Saudi leaders to accelerate expenditures and development.

Subsidized Consumption. With the large share of national income earned directly by the government, there has been relatively small direct subsidization of consumption by the government. The new plan envisages a major role for the government in improving the economic and social well-being of Saudi citizens. The continuance and major expansion of education and health care for all citizens without direct cost is merely an extension of past policies. The new plan, however, contains a proposal for an extensive social security program aimed at the essential requirements of all Saudis. Some foods are to be subsidized, housing is to be provided at subsidized rates, utility services are to be extended by the government and provided at lower rates, and a wide range of recreational and social programs are to be offered by the government. The government has accepted major responsibilities it did not have before, and it has increased the extent of already existing programs. These new responsibilities and program increases represent a potential commitment of resources of great proportions, given the lack of marketable skills and the low standard of living of many Saudis. As the rapid pace of development pushes up prices in such sectors as housing, the costs of many of these programs should be expected to rise considerably. Certainly the experience of Western countries suggests that this will be the case.

Some Remaining Problems and Issues

The development plan has its weaknesses, of course. Some of these weaknesses are recognized in the plan but left unresolved. Others are ignored. In this evaluation I will discuss only the major problems and issues raised by the development plan.

The Constraints. A rather short section, considering the length of the planning document, contains a remarkably frank statement about the major impediments to achieving the goals, programs, and projects stipulated by the plan:

> It is clear . . . that the financial cost of the Plan is not the critical measure of its size.
>
> The conclusion to be drawn from the projections of manpower requirements is not so clear. The forecast of private sector requirements is drawn mainly from estimates of the manpower that would be required given the projections of growth in value added in constant prices. These projections were based on an overall assessment of the highest rates of growth sustainable over the period of the Plan, taking into account the absorptive capacity of the economy. On the other hand, the public sector projections reflect the manpower estimated by government agencies as needed for the implementation of their plans. Hence the manpower projections already reflect to a considerable degree the limitations on absorptive capacity; nevertheless, even the increase in the work force specified above may prove exceedingly difficult to satisfy.
>
> It is recognized that to achieve an average annual rate of growth of 60 percent in construction volume will be exceedingly difficult however much success is achieved in improving construction methods and supplies. In view of this potential constraint on plan implementation, it may be necessary to reschedule construction programs from year to year in accordance with development priorities and in the light of the impact of growing construction volume on prices, wages, contract bids, services, supplies, and housing.
>
> Work has already started on an assessment of physical constraints on plan implementation. High priority must now be given to developing central planning capability to define priorities in relation to manpower and construction requirements and to rescheduling of lower priority projects and programs in the light of these constraints.[7]

If it were not for the fashionableness of five-year plans, this one might better have been labeled "1975–1985." The reservations about implementation are deserved. The planning process is still one in which projects and programs are compiled but not reconciled.

It is not evident how priorities are to be established. Since all projects and programs of the plan have been approved by the Council of Ministers, each ministry and agency has authority to proceed. In the manufacturing sector, not all licenses have been approved, but

---

[7] *Development Plan, 1975-1980,* p. 605.

given the importance attached to the industrial sector, the Saudi authorities may be hesitant to make cuts there.

Three decision variables may be used simultaneously. The projects of those agencies, ministries, and private firms best able to organize their projects and investments and to obtain the relatively scarce inputs are likely to be initiated first. Others will be delayed as their sponsors organize and attempt to acquire the necessary manpower and construction materials.

Some sections of the plan will tend to be neglected by default if not by design. The most likely section for neglect seems to be the allocations for municipalities. Because many of these can be delayed without interfering with the activities of productive sectors, there will be a natural tendency to allow them to fall to the bottom of any priority list. This is especially true for municipalities other than Riyadh, Jeddah, and those on the east coast in the new industrial centers.

Finally, projects associated with the hydrocarbon industrialization program are likely to get the highest priority. This will be true especially of those involving Petromin.

Inflation. One consequence of the ambitious targets of the plan will be to exacerbate the already persistent inflation. Prices of land, housing, and construction materials should rise much more rapidly than those of other products. Wage rates for skilled construction workers will likewise be raised quickly as competition for scarce inputs becomes heated. Thus, even though inflation is potentially less of a problem in Saudi Arabia than in other countries because there is no foreign exchange constraint and the Saudis have the rest of the world to bargain with and to buy from, the prices of the products and services mentioned above will be influenced less by imports during the next five years than will a wide range of other goods and services.

There is one major constraint on the use of imports as the escape valve for inflationary pressures. The plan reflects an anticipation of a 30 percent annual rate of growth of imports. At present, the ports of Jeddah and Dammam are the main points of entry for imports. As recently as 1973, the existing capacity of these two ports was approximately 4 million tons; imports amounted to approximately 3 million tons.[8] However, "the number of operational berths in Dammam . . . was more than doubled this year [1975], from six to fourteen."[9]

---

[8] Ibid., p. 507.

[9] *World Financial Markets*, Morgan Guaranty Trust Company of New York, October 20, 1975, p. 11.

The plan contains a projection that as much as 13 million tons will have to be imported annually by 1980. It is obviously conceivable that port facilities will be inadequate to process the material required by the projections of the plan. "The implementation of much of the second Plan depends on the ability of the ports to cope with this large inflow of goods. If they cannot, severe disruptions in the implementation schedule for the Plan as a whole must be anticipated." [10]

The ability to increase the tonnage handled by the ports does not depend entirely on increasing the physical capacity of the ports. The ports are operated inefficiently. It is assumed in the plan that improved handling of cargo could raise the capacity of the two major ports by approximately 6 million tons annually during the plan period. Under present conditions, the ports are a cause of uncertainty and delay; for that reason alone they contribute to increased costs and higher prices.

To sum up, inflationary pressures are likely to be considerable and to cause the prices of projects and social welfare programs to increase. If the rate of inflation is underestimated in the plan the financial requirements of implementing it are correspondingly underestimated. At the same time that a slow rate of project completion can reduce short-term financial requirements, the same factors that cause delays also cause prices to rise and thereby increase the financial requirements. It is not possible to predict the relative magnitudes of these two countervailing forces acting on total expenditures, but consideration of them does illustrate the fact that delay and postponement of projects do not result automatically in a greater budget surplus.

It is difficult to anticipate the way in which the Saudi authorities will react to severe inflationary pressures. The primary alternatives are to scale back the pace of the development effort, to resort to some system of wage and price controls, and to protect the Saudi consumer by subsidizing the prices of food, clothing, and housing. Regardless of which approaches are used, shortages are inevitable; given the administrative inexperience of the Saudi bureaucracy, it probably will be reluctant to resort to central allocation schemes or to a comprehensive system of wage and price controls. A combination of retarding implementation of the plan and providing subsidies to the consumer is likely to be seen as the only feasible approach to coping with the related problems of inflation and shortages. If projects can be delayed until the availability of physical resources and manpower

---

[10] *Development Plan, 1975-1980,* pp. 507-508.

has been demonstrated, the problems can be limited to some degree. Again, the failure to specify priorities in the plan contributes to its weakness as a planning document. The Saudis have yet to establish the authority necessary for reconciling competing claims on limited resources.

Saudi Foreign Investment. During the plan period, revenues will exceed expenditures. If the government should accumulate foreign-exchange assets approximating $100 billion by 1980, which seems reasonable, earnings on these investments might approach $10 billion a year by the end of the plan period. It might have been expected that the role of foreign assets in development strategy would have been considered in the plan. Income from foreign assets can be used to finance government expenditures. To the extent that one major purpose of the plan is to diversify sources of income and foreign exchange by reducing dependence upon the export of petroleum, one approach could be to diversify foreign-exchange assets, both geographically and by types of economic activity. In the formulation of development policies, there are trade-offs between income directed into domestic projects and income invested in foreign income-earning assets. The plan offers little insight into what these trade-offs might be or even any indication that they received much attention when the plan was drafted. The emphasis of the plan with respect to foreign assets seems to be only on maintaining a strong and fully convertible riyal. The emphasis is on managing foreign payments and receipts to enable the government to meet "all foreseeable needs and to enjoy a reserve balance adequate to meet unexpected contingencies." [11] Only a broad reference is made to the management of reserves according to income considerations. It is stated that the highest possible returns will be realized on financial capital "by management of financial reserves in accordance with a balanced assessment of the relative rates of return, security, and liquidity of different forms of investment." [12]

There are two possible explanations for the failure of the Saudis to integrate a foreign-investment program into the plan. First, authority for establishing investment strategy is vested in a committee at the ministerial level headed by Crown Prince Fahd. It is likely that this group's operations are independent of the planning process and that its deliberations and decisions are not subject to review by the planning authorities. The requirement of confidentiality in such

---

[11] Ibid., p. 80.
[12] Ibid., p. 86.

matters could be sufficient justification for this. Second, the Saudis may be reluctant to divulge their potential foreign-exchange assets. Other claimants, domestic and foreign, may increase their efforts to share the Saudi government wealth if that wealth accumulates as foreign assets. Throughout the plan there is evidence of a conscious effort to imply that financial resources will be absorbed by the domestic development program. But in fact, a defensive posture towards foreign-exchange assets is not warranted. These holdings can be an integral part of Saudi development strategy, and they can contribute both to government income and to national economic security.

The Saudis have been quite conservative in their attitudes toward economic security ever since King Faisal assumed the throne and control of fiscal affairs. In its first five-year plan, 1970–75, Saudi Arabia set a target of maintaining foreign-exchange reserves at a level equivalent to one-and-a-half-year's imports. This target level was viewed as protection against the vulnerability that ensues from reliance upon petroleum exports for revenues and income and on imports for maintaining consumption standards and development projects. As an investor, the Saudi government has maintained a high level of liquid foreign assets to protect itself against a decline in foreign-exchange earnings, whether this decline be self-initiated or imposed by others. It is therefore unreasonable to regard a large accumulation of liquid foreign assets merely as a residue of savings. The usefulness of these funds suggests that the Saudis will be prudent in their management and cannot afford to take capital losses in order to manipulate them for political purposes. Political manipulation would be more feasible if the funds were truly surplus and were not important in the promotion of economic stability and security. These funds are the Saudi equivalent of storage of petroleum in a country such as the United States. Each represents an attempt to reduce vulnerability to short-run disruptions in the supply of oil. When economic security is recognized as the goal, neither the storage of oil nor the holding of liquid foreign assets is a surplus in any accurate sense of the word. If imports should rise to the projected level of almost $20 billion by 1980, and if the Saudis should continue to hold liquid assets equivalent to one-and-one-half times that amount, these assets should evidently approach $35 billion. During the first two years of implementation of the plan, when imports should be at a much lower level, liquid foreign assets of the Saudi government should approach this total. By 1980, imports may be close to two-thirds—and certainly will be half—the anticipated levels of revenues from petroleum assumed in the development plan.

Besides the security and income provided by liquid foreign assets, foreign exchange savings provide the Saudis with an option of investing perhaps as much as $65 billion in long-term assets. The primary motive behind such investments should be maximization of income with the usual consideration for the safety of assets. It is not likely that investments in longer-term assets would have the purpose of securing equity control. The Saudis do not have the administrative capacity to involve themselves extensively in the management of foreign enterprises, and they will undoubtedly try to avoid the political responses that would ensue if they obtained control over major businesses in other countries. Purchases of corporate and government bonds and of stocks involving less than 10 percent of equity would be more likely to be feasible than purchases involving "control." The Saudi government, avoiding "control," could diversify its assets by country and by industry. Given the capital requirements in North America, Western Europe, and Japan, the Saudis should have no difficulty placing the available volume of funds.

It is a weakness of the planning process, rather than of the plan itself, that these options are not included in the development plan. There is no indication that the Saudi authorities are prepared to compare the costs of pressing forward in implementing the projects and programs set forth in the plan with the returns from foreign assets. If implementation of the plan is pushed ahead at all costs, more efficient alternative ways of generating and diversifying income may be forgone. This will be more likely in the short run, when the rate of implementation of the plan may be slower.

Services. While the emphasis of the plan is on the development of the industrial sector, the organization and growth of services is of utmost importance to the Saudi economy. The reason the development plan gives less attention to services, of course, is that it is primarily private, and the government has little direct responsibility for its activities. Development of physical infrastructure is important to the functioning of service activities, but the relationship is an indirect one and one not emphasized in the plan.

Private services include wholesale and retail trade, transportation, real estate and finance, and personal services. Overall, the average annual rate of growth between 1970 and 1975 was almost 13 percent; the rate is expected to climb to 15 percent during 1976–80. Most important, the employment of more than 1.2 million persons by 1980 in the services, including commerce, is projected. Since it is expected that there will be no more than 600,000 employed in construction and 77,000 in manufacturing, services is of overwhelming importance as a source of employment.

Services should be recognized as important to the development program. Service activities will introduce those Saudis with a minimum of education and skills to a modern economy. Unlike manufacturing, services are labor-intensive and can provide employment for large numbers of workers. Anyone who has shopped in the native market (suq) can attest to the Saudi's adeptness at retail trade, a type of economic activity consistent with the traditions and beliefs of the Saudis, particularly the Bedouin, who tend to look down upon manual labor or any activity that involves working with one's hands.

The encouragement and development of services is consistent with and essential to all the other programs designed to maintain earnings from foreign exchange. Whether foreign exchange is earned from exports of crude oil, exports of the products of a substantial hydrocarbon industrial complex, or as income from foreign assets, earnings will be used to finance the wide range of imports—food, clothing, home furnishings, home appliances, automobiles, recreational equipment—that will be brought into the kingdom. Service businesses will also maintain and repair these. In a fundamental way, services will be the key determinant of the extent to which oil revenue is translated into a better standard of living for the Saudi citizen. The observer of Saudi development plans and of their implementation should be aware of all this.

The Risks of Industrialization. Feasibility studies for individual projects are conducted by the ministry or organization having jurisdiction over the sector of the economy to which the project belongs. Petromin has had the responsibility for evaluating the economic feasibility of the hydrocarbon complexes that are to be built. The central planners have had little to say about the relative merits of the proposals.

There is ample reason for assuming the economic feasibility of these projects. At present, 87 percent of the natural gas produced is flared. Natural gas liquids are in short supply throughout the world and are likely to remain so for the foreseeable future. What is less certain is the future market for an assortment of chemicals, including ethylene, ammonia, and methanol, products that are to be produced in substantial quantities in Saudi Arabia.

The major problem facing this segment of industry is that, along with the capacity existing and planned in North America and Western

Europe, additional capacity is being installed in most of the Arab oil-producing states and Iran. Each of the latter can anticipate a comparative advantage in the petrochemical industry, but for the group as a whole it is possible that more capacity will be installed than the market will bear at profitable prices. Also, petroleum refining and petrochemical installations are large complexes, requiring experienced management. The commitment of large amounts of relatively scarce investment resources, not in the form of financial capital but as import capacity, construction materials, and labor, will carry a heavy cost if the complexes are not successful after they are put on stream. This is especially true when consideration is given to the relatively small contribution of these projects to employment opportunities.

Perhaps we should applaud the Saudis for demonstrating that governments are capable of being risk takers. From the viewpoint of assessing the plan, however, we may question whether these projects are economically feasible and represent the best approach to diversifying sources of foreign exchange.

A Welfare State? The Saudis have usually maintained that they prefer not to duplicate the Kuwaiti experience with its emphasis on a substantial welfare program. In the plan they assert that only minimum standards will be guaranteed by government actions and programs. Yet, when the total of social programs, including subsidization of food staples, is added up, it is difficult to differentiate between the system which seems to be emerging in Saudi Arabia and that which exists in Kuwait. With education and health care provided by the government at no charge, with housing, transportation, electricity, and food subsidized, and with extensive social security programs to be in effect, the Saudi Arabian government is evidently assuming a major role in the economic life of its citizens.

With large revenues being earned by the state, the government has little reason to avoid such responsibilities. Saudi Arabia, with its larger population and more varied resources, has more scope for providing productive employment for its citizens than does Kuwait. But with economic welfare in the kingdom dependent upon the revenues from petroleum in the foreseeable future, it seems natural for the government to share this wealth through welfare programs. It is still too early to make judgments about the direction and scope of future Saudi welfare programs; their relative importance will help to shape the course of development in the kingdom and are elements of policy that will be important to observe in the coming years.

5
CONSEQUENCES AND POLICY IMPLICATIONS

Much in the development process being initiated in Saudi Arabia that is of major consequence to the Saudis themselves is also of major consequence to persons throughout the world, particularly in the industrialized countries. In this concluding chapter the major consequences of the large revenues of the Saudis and of their development plans will be assessed, and some policy implications for the United States will be discussed.

The Consequences

Saudi Attitudes toward Revenues. The most interesting consequence of Saudi development strategy lies in Saudi policies toward the volume and price of crude oil. It was noted in Chapter 1 that Saudi Arabia has the reserves and the capacity to vary the levels of its production and exports of crude oil more than does any other major petroleum exporter. The principal question is whether the Saudi development plan puts pressures on Saudi Arabia to maintain its high value of revenues, say in the range of $20 billion to $30 billion. The question to be answered is: If market pressures were tending to force down the price of OPEC oil (as indeed they are), to what extent would Saudi Arabia be willing to reduce the volume of its production and sales, and thus of its revenues, in order to maintain the OPEC target price? The answer depends on a range of circumstances, many of them outside the scope of this study. I consider the question only insofar as the answer to it is affected by the development plan and development strategy. Even with one's view of it thus restricted the question is a difficult one to answer.

The program of expenditures for the five years requires revenues of almost $30 billion a year, not including aid to other Arab and

Moslem countries and to internationally organized aid programs, for no accounting is given in the plan of the possible levels of such aid. Even if the plan were to be taken at face value, however, it is clear that Saudi Arabia could not afford a sustained decline in petroleum revenues. If Saudi Arabia were to reduce its oil output by 1 million barrels a day, assuming net revenues a barrel to be $10, the annual cost in revenues would be more than $3.5 billion. For example, 8 million barrels a day at $10 a barrel provides more than $29 billion in revenues; 7 million barrels a day provides $25.5 billion; 6 million barrels a day, $21.9 billion; 5 million barrels a day, $18.3 billion. (It must be remembered that these calculations assume a constant price throughout the stipulated range of output.)

It is reported that "Saudi Arabia has been told by the Stanford Research Institute, one of its consultants [the principal consultant to the Central Planning Organization], that it could cut oil production to three million barrels a day from the current seven million and still have income to pay for its huge development plans. In addition, by drawing on monetary reserves, the institute figured, the Saudis could cut to one million barrels a day." [1]

These statements are difficult to evaluate without knowing the price of oil assumed with each level of output. Consider the alternatives:

Revenues per barrel (dollars)	Annual revenues (billions of dollars)	
	3 million b/d	1 million b/d
10	11.2	3.7
12	13.4	4.4
14	15.4	5.1
16	17.6	5.8

No one can forecast with confidence the price of oil associated with various levels of output. If the reduction in Saudi Arabia's output corresponded to similar reductions on the part of other members of OPEC, then it would be reasonable to expect, during the five-year period of the plan, that prices could easily go to $16 a barrel. On the other hand, if reductions in Saudi Arabia's output were an isolated phenomenon, it is possible that the price per barrel would not change much. Demand conditions would also play a role. Generalizations about the price of oil at different levels of output for Saudi Arabia are thus not warranted.

Another key variable in determining the compatibility of reduced revenues with requirements under the plan is the length of any period

<hr>

[1] *Newsweek*, September 1, 1975, p. 13.

of declining revenues that might come about. The plan could probably accommodate short-run reductions taking place for two or three months, whereas if revenues should decline substantially for a year or more, reductions in revenues could seriously jeopardize the plan. The time dimension is also important in considering the willingness of Saudi Arabia to draw down monetary reserves. In the next two years, even though monetary reserves are at the relatively high level of about $40 billion as of the end of 1975, Saudi Arabia might be quite reluctant to reduce reserves. By 1980, assuming a greater accumulation of reserves, there might be more leeway for the Saudi authorities to finance expenditures by reducing reserves.[2] In either case, depletion of international financial reserves over an extended period would not seem to be a good policy.

The possible range of responses is great, and simply to talk about the scores of possibilities is not useful. If Saudi Arabia should be willing to junk its development program, much lower revenues could be tolerated. It does not seem likely, however, that Saudi Arabia would abandon its plan in midstream. Rather, determining the level of revenues consistent with the implementation of the plan would be a more useful approach in the attempt to anticipate Saudi actions.

Bottlenecks, primarily in construction and imports, will reduce expenditures far below those projected by the development plan. Especially during the next two or three years, the Saudis will do well to spend as much as $15 billion a year. Given the accumulation of financial reserves that has already occurred, Saudi Arabia might be content to watch revenues decline below $20 billion, believing that the development effort was not being compromised. If expenditures were cut substantially in areas other than productive investment, then even a smaller level of revenues could be tolerated. But given the expenditures that have been planned, any expectation that the Saudis might allow revenues to decline below $10 billion does not seem plausible, although it seems reasonable to conclude that Saudi Arabia might allow revenues to fall annually to $10 to $12 billion during the next few years. This implies a production level of about 3 million barrels a day if the price of oil should be in the range of $10–$12 a barrel.

It appears that the programs of the development plan can be carried out at an acceptable pace without putting Saudi Arabia into

---

[2] One can only conjecture about the ability of Saudi Arabia to draw on its reserves if the reason for a very low level of output, say one million b/d, is that oil is being used as a political weapon. If economic warfare is being waged, foreign assets of Saudi Arabia could be frozen in retaliation, or there might be an extreme response of confiscation.

the position of being less cooperative with OPEC than it has been so far and breaking the price of oil by attempting to increase revenues through increased output and sales. If Saudi Arabia could reconcile the requirements of the plan with an output of 3 million barrels a day, there would be no reason to believe that the policies of OPEC face a near-term threat from this quarter. The overall price tag of $143 billion on the development plan is misleading in this regard. Many programs and projects can be delayed or scrapped without interfering with the guts of the development program. Others will be delayed because of problems in organizing them and in obtaining materials and labor.

In reaching these judgments, statements from Saudi Arabian authorities are not very useful. On the one hand, the financial requirements of the entire development plan are often emphasized. These suit the Saudi desire to emphasize the fact that the kingdom can utilize all the revenues that are being earned. As was noted earlier, such a posture reduces pressures on Saudi Arabia to share its income and wealth and makes it more difficult for the other members of OPEC to get Saudi Arabia to bear the brunt of prorated reductions in production. At other times, the Saudis want to stress their economic and political independence by asserting that they can reduce their production and revenues without harming their development effort. The result is conflicting statements, and neither represents an accurate description of the Saudi situation.

Dependence upon the Foreign Sector. The development program aims at reducing the dependence of the economy upon petroleum exports. It appears that the development plan does little to reduce such reliance, however, and it increases dependence upon the foreign sector in other respects.

For a considerable period of time Saudi Arabia will be importing goods, particularly capital goods, upon which the entire development program depends. Virtually all of the hardware for the industrialization process must be imported. Also, if the rising monetary incomes of Saudis are to have an appreciable effect on their levels of living, goods and services must be imported from abroad to satisfy the increased consumer demand. Any disruption of the flow of imports, whether a result of political or of economic factors, would be in turn disruptive to the economy with respect to both consumption and investment. Second, the dependence upon imported labor for the next ten or fifteen years increases reliance upon the foreign sector. It is possible that U.S. citizens working in Saudi Arabia may number more than 50,000 by 1980. To maintain the total estimated foreign labor force of more than 800,000 in 1980 will require a high degree of political and economic stability. It is doubtful that the Saudis can attract skilled workers if economic relations between Saudi Arabia and the industrialized nations are subject to substantial tension. The workers must be assured, too, of their ability to transfer their earnings to their home country. Third, the encouragement of foreign investment in Saudi Arabia increases reliance on the foreign sector. In addition to the necessity of bringing in personnel from abroad, sources of spare parts and repair facilities must be available. Foreign firms will be repatriating profits and capital after operations become profitable. Fourth, Saudi Arabia is going to be a major financial investor in world markets. Saudi Arabia is already the third largest holder of foreign-exchange reserves in the world. With financial assets held throughout the world, Saudi Arabia acquires a strong vested interest in international financial stability.

Is it possible that Saudi Arabia could reduce this dependence considerably? Given the structure of the Saudi economy, it seems not to be possible. No feasible development strategy offers much likelihood of reducing these influences. A perpetuation of the reliance on exports of crude oil would not have such an effect. Only if Saudi Arabia chose not to develop and to accept the lower level of living associated with a traditional economy would the country be able to turn its back on the rest of the world and maintain itself as it did before the advent of growing oil revenues. Any feasible course of economic development aiming at modernization and major increases in real national product and income would have the same effect of increasing reliance upon the foreign sector. And it seems impossible to conceive of Saudi Arabia's turning off the faucet and deliberately choosing to maintain the relatively isolated condition that can be achieved only by accepting low levels of income. In any event, this clearly is not the choice that is inherent in the new development plan.

Private Wealth. Thus far, attention has been focused on the income and wealth of the government. One major consequence of the reliance upon private property and the market system, however, is that the large government revenues will quickly be transformed into private wealth. Much of the private wealth will be held by private Saudi citizens, but some favored non-Saudis will also gain. All wholesale and retail trade will be carried on in the private sector. Much of the purchasing done by the government, directly or indirectly, will be funneled through the private sector. The salaries of government employees will be quickly spent in private markets. In such a setting, franchises and import licenses can lead to great wealth. As one example, it is a short process by which the petroleum revenues of the Saudi government become income for the Riyadh Mercedes dealer. The rapid expansion of consumption expenditures that accompanies the higher petroleum incomes will generate wealth for many private businessmen, particularly those engaged in imports. The disposition of their wealth will be important to the future development of the Saudi economy and to other countries as well. There will be many more names added to those of Gaith Pharaon and Adnan Khashoggi, both of whom have already made their mark in U.S. financial markets. Gaith Pharaon, whose father was foreign adviser to King Faisal, was active in the purchase into the Bank of the Commonwealth in Detroit by a group of Saudis, and he also is a leading figure in the Arabian Maritime Transport Company. These two men and others like the bin Ladins, the el Gossaibis, the Ali Rezas, and the bin Zaghers may become as well known in the coming decade as such names as Gould and Onassis have been known in their times. Studies of the international financial impact of the large foreign-exchange savings of the OPEC countries have concentrated on government savings. This emphasis is justified, because it is the centralized control of these assets that makes them potentially destabilizing. It is private wealth, however, that is more likely to be directed into equity investment, and policy issues concerning foreign ownership of U.S. assets will eventually focus on the acquisition of assets by private individuals in countries belonging to OPEC. Because of its large revenues and its reliance upon the private sector, Saudi Arabia will spawn more than its share of major private investors. Similarly, commercial banking groups in Saudi Arabia or regionally based banks with strong Saudi interests will accumulate extensive financial resources. In the coming decade they are likely to exert appreciable influence in international financial markets.

International Investment. Saudi Arabia will emerge during the balance of the 1970s as one of the major international investors. Some of its investments will be made by the government and some will be on private account. The amount will be substantial, but there is little on which to base a precise estimate of Saudi private investment abroad during this period. This investment will be placed in many forms and will likely go to markets over the world, although North America, Europe, and Japan will be its principal recipients. It will be placed by individual Saudis, by groups of Saudis functioning as investment companies or banks, and by consortia of Saudis aligned with other interests. To trace the source of funds will be difficult, and often the Saudi share will not be separately identifiable. As an example, a proposal was made to form a commercial bank, UBAF Arab American Bank, in New York. The bank has applied for membership in the Federal Reserve System.[3] The partners are Bankers Trust New York Corporation; First Chicago Corporation; Security Pacific Corporation, Los Angeles; Texas Commerce Bancshares Inc., Houston; Arab American Bank, Cairo; the Central Bank of Egypt; Union des Banques Arabes et Françaises; UBAF Ltd., London; UBAN-Arab Japanese Finance Ltd., Hong Kong; Union des Banques Arabes et Européenes, Luxembourg; Unione di Banche Arabe ed Europee (Italia) S.p.A., Rome; Alahli Bank of Kuwait; Arab Bank Ltd., Jordan; Libyan Arab Foreign Bank; Banque du Maroc, Morocco; Commercial Bank of Syria; National Bank of Abu Dhabi; Central Bank of Oman; Sudan Commercial Bank, Khartoum; and Riyadh Bank Ltd., Saudi Arabia. With such a proliferation of firms, any attempt to trace the sources of funds associated with these enterprises over a period of time would be highly unlikely to succeed. But we can be sure that billions of dollars will in time have been invested in banking, real estate, private and public bonds, and equities.

Investment of government funds will be more easily identifiable and more easily estimated, even though projections of dollar value of such investment are somewhat speculative. Few would doubt that in the absence of a drastic slowdown of petroleum production and revenues, the government of Saudi Arabia will have at least $50 billion in foreign-exchange savings by 1980; the figure may be as much as $100 billion.[4] By the end of 1975, Saudi Arabian foreign-reserve assets were approximately $40 billion.[5] Foreign-exchange savings would have to average $14 billion a year during the period of the plan to reach $100 billion by 1980.

International reserves of the government have grown rapidly (see Table 11). Until now, for the most part, the Saudis have placed their holdings in short-term assets other than equities. Certificates of deposit and short-term government securities are the typical outlets. To the surprise of some observers, the Saudi government has not become a major purchaser of gold, although there may be considerable

---

[3] *Wall Street Journal*, August 20, 1975.

[4] Donald Wells, *Saudi Arabian Revenues and Expenditures: The Potential for Foreign Exchange Savings* (Washington, D.C.: Resources for the Future, 1974), p. 29.

[5] International Monetary Fund, *International Financial Statistics*, March 1976, p. 331.

Table 11

EXTERNAL ASSETS OF THE GOVERNMENT, 1970–75
(millions of dollars)

End of Year	Gold	Foreign Exchange [a]	Foreign Investments [a]	Total
1970	165	838	226	1,229
1971	165	1,589	220	1,974
1972	165	3,121	283	3,569
1973	157	3,773	661	4,591
1974	157	16,257	5,795	22,209
1975 [b]	126	n.a.	n.a.	37,862

[a] The Saudi Arabia Monetary Agency differentiates between "foreign exchange" and "foreign investments," but the two categories are indistinguishable in practice and both may be considered as short-term assets. Demand-deposit working balances are kept quite small.

[b] November 1975.

Sources: Central Planning Organization, *Development Plan, 1975–1980*, p. 40; IMF, *International Financial Statistics*, March 1976, p. 331.

amounts of gold bought on private account by Saudis. For the oil-exporting countries as a group, the largest proportion of the funds have been invested in the Eurodollar market and in the United States, with smaller amounts going to Great Britain.

Through 1975, Saudi Arabia engaged in very little long-term investment of its surplus funds. Traditionally, the government had viewed its foreign-exchange savings as a hedge against declines in petroleum revenues. The aim under the 1970–75 plan was a ratio of foreign-exchange assets to imports of 1.5:1. At a time when revenues fluctuated considerably from year to year—especially after the experience of the late 1950s, when foreign-exchange assets were depleted—the desire to maintain such a high level of foreign reserves is understandable and the maintenance of such a level is prudent. If annual imports should rise to a level of $15 billion to $20 billion, the ratio of reserve assets to imports could be maintained by purchasing up to $35 billion worth of short-term assets. While imports cannot be accurately forecast, any reasonable estimate of Saudi demand for short-term assets based on considerations of liquidity is not likely to exceed $35 billion or $40 billion. Foreign-exchange savings of the Saudi government are likely to be at least twice that amount by 1980; the Saudi authorities therefore have considerable discretion in the disposition of these funds. With liquidity requirements met, it is likely that the Saudi authorities will attempt to invest primarily on the basis of anticipated income. Saudi Arabia's role as a major exporter of capital into international financial markets will depend partly on the types of investments chosen and their geographical distribution.

There has been no clear statement from the Saudis concerning their investment strategy. As early as 1973 a ministerial committee, headed by Crown Prince Fahd, was established to work out government policy with respect to foreign investment. The deaths of King Faisal and of Anwar Ali, the head of the Saudi Arabian Monetary Agency for fifteen years and the most trusted and respected financial adviser to the throne, undoubtedly have made the task of working out the policy more difficult and have delayed the process. The Saudis are surely sensitive, too, about the public response in the United States and elsewhere to the potential takeover of industries by the Arabs. It is likely that whatever policies are adopted will be carried out discreetly and that publicity will be avoided as much as possible.

While not explicitly a part of the development plan, foreign investments for income would support the emphasis of the Saudis on diversified sources of income. Given the limits of size and the stage of development of Saudi Arabia, investments in a range of industries and in many different countries offer a faster route to diversification than do domestic programs. It has already been argued that Saudi Arabia cannot escape a reliance on the foreign sector; foreign investments should not be rejected for that reason. The reasons that foreign investment is not thus far an integral part of the development plan are probably jurisdictional considerations within the government and the desire to preserve the confidentiality of investment policies and decisions.

For obvious reasons, the conscious utilization of capital exports as a device to promote economic development is not much discussed in the literature on economic development. There the focus is on capital imports as a means of acquiring a scarce factor of production. When funds have accumulated in Saudi Arabia in the amounts that are expected, the Saudis can choose between the gains to national development from investing domestically or investing in other countries. At one extreme, Saudi Arabia could have chosen to rely upon crude oil and income from the government's foreign investments to subsidize imports of consumer goods. Economic activity in this case would have been concentrated in the trade and service sectors. Clearly Saudi Arabia has not chosen this course. Foreign investments beyond considerations of international liquidity will originate from a residue of funds that could not be spent. But regardless of the rationale for foreign investments, it remains in the interests of Saudi Arabia to maximize investment income to whatever extent is consistent with concern for the security of the investments. What investment strategy might emerge?

First, it is doubtful that the government would want to acquire majority or total control of many of the equity investments it might undertake. Saudi Arabia does not have enough citizens with managerial and financial training to want to divert them to the conduct of affairs of businesses abroad. All the available talent of this sort will be needed to deal with the management of domestic operations. Second, the Saudis will want to avoid the political responses that would be likely to follow the acquisition of equity control over corporations in such countries as the United States. Therefore, longer-term investments are likely to consist of equity investments not involving control, corporate bonds, and long-term government securities.

The Saudis are likely to believe themselves most secure operating in government security markets. Most important, there is unlikely to be any foreign political concern over purchases of government securities. The power of the debtor is likely to be greater than that of the creditor in most instances, in contrast to the situation in which an individual corporation would have to cope with the financial resources of an entire government. The Saudi government has had experience with government security markets and for the near term is likely to feel more comfortable with government securities. One should not minimize the difficulty of studying the desirability and feasibility of major new investments and then of reaching a policy consensus. Saudi Arabia may continue to distribute its investment funds abroad as it has in the past primarily out of the inertia that comes because of the press of other business.

The Balance of Payments. The Saudi Arabian balance of international payments was dominated by three accounts in the early 1970s. Exports of petroleum on current account were the principal source of international receipts. Payments for imports of goods and services were about one-fourth to one-fifth the level of current-accounts receipts, but the largest payments account was investment income, which in 1973 was equal to more than one-third of international receipts. Nearly all investment income payments were profits repatriated by Aramco. On current account during this period, there was an export surplus that averaged about one-fourth of total current-account receipts. Most of this surplus was channeled into gold, foreign-exchange holdings, and investments of the Saudi Arabian central bank. By 1973, however, net private holdings of foreign assets, which amounted to less than $250 million in 1972, reached the level of $1 billion.[6]

During the next five years the structure of the Saudi balance of payments should change considerably. Reduced profit margins for Aramco and 60 percent ownership of the facilities by the Saudi government (increasing to 100 percent soon) will reduce investment-income payments in the oil sector. In the longer run, investment-income payments will grow rapidly and outstrip the income payments going to Aramco, because the widespread participation of foreign companies will eventually generate profits for repatriation. However, since a gestation period will be needed for putting these investments into place and establishing operations, investment-income payments are likely to decline for the next two or three years. Particularly in the hydrocarbons sector, investments may not produce income for four or five years. The reduction of investment-income payments will be offset to some extent by the repatriation of wages and salaries earned by the foreign labor force.

Another major change will be the growing importance of income earned by the Saudi government and private investors on their foreign assets. In a few years income on investment receipts may be a major factor in the current account. These receipts will be an important factor in helping to maintain the current-account surplus regardless of the rapid rise in payments for import. The current-account surplus should remain substantial for the next five years. Those who attempt to measure this surplus must take into account not only government income on investments but also income on private investments. The latter is difficult to forecast, but should be substantial.

One result will be a strong position for the Saudi riyal. It is likely that the value of the Saudi riyal will appreciate against the other major currencies: indeed, the riyal has appreciated about 16 percent against the dollar since 1972. Since it is likely that any future increases in the price of oil will not be major ones, appreciation of their currency may be one way that the Saudis can at least partially maintain the real income of their oil receipts. Saudi Arabia's strong balance-of-payments position and its strong currency will help to protect its real income.

---

[6] *Development Plan, 1975-1980*, p. 32.

The Implications for United States Policy

Saudi Arabia has initiated an ambitious development program that will shape the country's economic institutions and the structure of its economy. It is useful for U.S. policy makers to examine this program and its implications for U.S. policies toward energy in general and petroleum imports in particular. Saudi development policies and programs can be only one of the considerations that goes into the making of U.S. policies. At the same time, however, the economic policies of Saudi Arabia condition the attitudes of the Saudi government toward petroleum revenues and that which underlies them, price and the quantity of output. Saudi Arabian responses to changing market conditions for oil will vary according to the perceived importance of revenues. The more important revenue considerations are, the less freedom Saudi Arabia has to use oil as a political weapon.

Certain characteristics of the Saudi development program that are important from the perspective of U.S. policy makers are these:

• It is an ambitious program. The Saudis have chosen to begin a rapid industrialization process.

• Delays in implementation will cause expenditures to fall behind those forecasted in the plan.

• The program relies upon foreign labor and foreign enterprises, particularly in the industrial sector.

• During the next five years, the development program will result in little change in the structure of the Saudi economy and its dependence upon exports of crude oil as a source of income.

• A high level of capital exports will accompany the development program.

Two somewhat contradictory results emerge. First, Saudi Arabia retains its ability to accept a considerable variation in its revenues without jeopardizing the development program. This flexibility strengthens the chances that Saudi Arabia will be able to protect its own development objectives while at the same time helping OPEC to maintain the high price of oil. During the period of the plan it would appear that no pressures upon Saudi Arabia to break with OPEC will be generated by its own development objectives.[7] Second, Saudi Arabia has undertaken a program that is highly dependent upon

---

[7] This does not mean that Saudi Arabia might be unwilling to reduce petroleum output for other reasons. For example, Saudi Arabia might balk at reducing production if other producers attempted to maintain their production levels or if Saudi Arabia were to become concerned about OPEC's abilities to prop up the *future* price of oil.

goods, services, technology, and manpower from the industrialized countries of the West and Japan. The industrialization process, particularly in the hydrocarbon sector, will take between five and ten years to complete, and if the supply of goods and personnel were to be disrupted during this period, the industrialization program would be jeopardized.

U.S. policy should attempt to facilitate the implementation of the Saudi development plan. The United States and other major oil importers have a strong interest in maintaining a stable flow of petroleum from Saudi Arabia and the other major oil exporters. This interest can be advanced if such a country as Saudi Arabia has a like interest in maintaining imports of goods and labor as part of the implementation of its development plan. Industrialization will help to integrate the Saudi economy into the world economy, and it will also create a vested interest in the stability of existing international economic institutions. The increased wealth of Saudi Arabia also contributes to such a vested interest. The greater the wealth, the greater the cost of disruption and instability. One of the results of the rapid Saudi Arabian industrialization program is that the employment and incomes of increasing numbers of Saudis will become dependent upon the continued development of these industries, and disruptions will have direct effects on them.

The development program also is a key to the recycling of dollars earned as petroleum revenues. United States exports to Saudia Arabia have increased substantially in recent years. Total Saudi imports increased 49 percent in 1972 and approximately 55 percent each year in 1973 and 1974. For the first quarter of 1975, Saudi Arabian imports from OECD countries were more than one-and-one-half times those of the first quarter of 1973. U.S. exports to Saudi Arabia doubled in 1972, increased 40 percent in 1973, and nearly doubled again in 1974.[8] With the growing participation of U.S. firms in the development program, U.S. exports to Saudi Arabia should be expected to expand considerably during the next five years. Saudi salary payments to U.S. citizens working in Saudi Arabia and income on investments earned by U.S. firms located in Saudi Arabia should also grow rapidly and swell the flow of dollars back to the United States. In earnings, the United States will benefit from the Saudi development program probably more than will any of the other industrialized countries. There is no need for the United States to subsidize this process. It is sufficient that the Saudis have access to markets. The United States

---

[8] Morgan Guaranty Trust Company of New York, *World Financial Markets*, January 21, 1975, p. 7.

should not do anything to obstruct the flow of goods and services and personnel.

This policy should also apply to the flow of financial capital from Saudi Arabia to the United States. Studies to determine the circumstances in which foreign investment is detrimental to U.S. national security are warranted. Control of defense-oriented industries is obviously a legitimate reason for concern about foreign ownership. However, as we argued earlier, the Saudi Arabian government is unlikely to engage in much equity-control investment, and there is no evidence yet that they intend to do so. Except for considerations of national security, Saudi financial investments in the United States should be encouraged. To do so is consistent with efforts to relieve a growing concern about the availability of capital to meet the investment requirements of the U.S. economy during the coming decade. Even if most of Saudi investments were to be directed into the government securities market it would help to release other funds for private ventures. It is in the interest of the United States to foster mutual interests. For Saudi Arabia to have a major financial stake in the United States would be one way of accomplishing this goal.

Conclusion. Saudi Arabia has initiated a plan for development that envisages a high rate of investment and rapid economic growth. The response of the Saudis to the opportunities that are afforded by the kingdom's new level of wealth has thus far been an attempt to provide new bases for employment and more diversified sources of income, particularly in industry. A few years ago no one could have anticipated the scale and pace at which modernization would be attempted.

The massive program of development seems to have been adopted without any careful comparison of the benefits from beginning projects with the benefits from delaying their start until the shortages of skilled personnel and imported materials are less severe. The reason seems to be that, politically, the planning authorities in Saudi Arabia would have found it difficult to resist either the pressures from the various ministries to undertake their programs or the more general pressures of the Saudi population to share in the new wealth. The Saudis have struck it rich, and their attitudes are more likely to resemble those of a boom town during a gold rush than those of a nation carefully and prudently husbanding its resources.

Delays that center on construction and imports will cause actual expenditures to fall far short of planned expenditures during the period from 1975 to 1980. Inflation will be severe throughout these five years. Since there are no clear-cut priorities for projects, moreover, it is unlikely that individual projects will be postponed entirely until resources are available; rather, most projects are likely to be extended over longer periods than those anticipated by the development plan. Completion of projects is likely to depend on the relative efficiency and political influence of individual ministries and on the skills of the foreign contractors in obtaining the necessary resources. Industrial projects in the hydrocarbon sector and those controlled by the Ministry of Defense are likely to be managed best. Municipal projects, such as those attempting to improve housing, transportation, and communication in the cities, are less likely to fare well.

There seems to be little that Saudi Arabia can do to decrease its economic dependence on international trade and finance. Expenditures on foreign contractors, foreign workers, and imports will rise substantially. Even though Saudi Arabia's expenditures will not be as great as its oil revenues, Saudi imports of goods and services will help to recycle a large proportion of earnings from petroleum exports. Most of the Saudi expenditures on imports are likely to be to industrialized countries, because those countries are best able to supply the types of products and services required by the development plan.

While Saudi Arabia also emerges from recent developments as a major exporter of financial capital, there seems no reason to doubt that international financial markets will be able to absorb the approximately $100 billion that the kingdom is projected to invest between 1975 and 1980. It appears that Saudi Arabia has done little to integrate the disposition of these funds with the development planning process in general. Income from financial investments abroad seems to be an efficient way to diversify Saudi sources of income and revenue, and perhaps in the future the Ministry of Planning will be given new authority to compare the benefits from a domestic expenditure with those from a foreign investment. The current development plan is the weaker for not having made such comparisons.

Saudi Arabia's efforts at development are consistent with the interests of the United States. As it becomes better integrated into the world economy, Saudi Arabia is likely to acquire the same sort of vested interests in international economic stability that other rich countries have. The United States is becoming a major trading partner of Saudi Arabia, both in exports and in imports, and both countries will gain from this growth in trade. There is a similar growth in international financial investment between the two countries. The increases in both trade and investment have come about from market forces; they have not and do not require special arrangements and inducements. While political developments in the Middle East could interrupt these economic relationships, the potential for political disruption should not obscure the mutual benefits from trade and investment. A development strategy of Saudi Arabia that emphasizes large and immediate expenditures lessens the chances of recurrence of the sort of economic problems that arose as a consequence of the fourfold increase in the price of oil in 1973–74. For the most part United States policies seem to recognize these mutual interests, and future policies of the United States should do nothing to discourage the current attitudes of Saudi Arabia toward the disposition of its new wealth.